A Precept Bible Study for Home Groups

ACTS

The Birth of the Church

A Verse-by-Verse Journey through the book of Acts

Ralph Robert Gomez

ISBN 978-1-63885-279-7 (Paperback)
ISBN 978-1-63885-282-7 (Digital)

Scripture quotations taken from the (NASB®)
New American Standard Bible®, Copyright © 1960, 1971, 1977,
1995, 2020 by The Lockman Foundation.
Used by permission.
All rights reserved. www.lockman.org.

Scripture quotations taken from the (NIV®)
New International Version®, NIV®. Copyright ©1973, 1978, 1984, 2011 by Biblica, Inc.™
Used by permission of Zondervan.
All rights reserved worldwide. www.zondervan.com.
The "NIV" and "New International Version" are trademarks registered
in the United States Patent and Trademark Office by Biblica, Inc.™

Scripture quotations marked MSG are taken from THE MESSAGE,
copyright © 1993, 2002, 2018 by Eugene H. Peterson.
Used by permission of NavPress,
represented by Tyndale House Publishers. All rights reserved.

A special thank you to GotQuestions.org for the content,
as it was of great benefit to me in writing this book.

Disclaimer
The views and conclusions of this study guide are based on the author's in-depth study of the book of Acts.
The author understands that others may come to different conclusions based on their own study.
All scripture quotations are taken from the NASB® unless otherwise
marked. Emphasis has been added throughout the book.

Covenant Books
11661 Hwy 707
Murrells Inlet, SC 29576
www.covenantbooks.com

PRAISE FOR

Acts: The Birth of the Church

Ralph Gomez's verse-by-verse study on the book of Acts is outstanding! It is packed with great information and engaging discussion questions that get you thinking "outside the box." This study will not only inform you, but it will also challenge you to grow! I would strongly encourage anyone to take this amazing journey through the book of Acts.

MICHAEL CARDENAS
Executive Pastor
Legacy Christian Fellowship

This is a very well thought out and organized Bible study guide through the book of Acts. Ralph has laid out the information in a very organized and easy way to follow. Any believer at any level should be able to benefit from this study guide.

I like that this verse-by-verse guide has you methodically observed the passage in order to "digest" and understand what it is saying. Additionally, Ralph has added a couple of very beneficial features, such as a section marked "Commentary" that gives very beneficial explanation of the text to help the Bible student understand the background of the passage. Likewise, I love the "Re-Read" section at the end of the chapter. This is a "nice" twist that I have not seen used in other study guides. But I love the idea of rereading the passage you just studied but, this time, with all of the background and understanding you gained having gone through the study guide. I believe rereading the passage after you've studied will be very eye-opening for the student of the Scriptures.

PAUL BOUTAN
Senior Pastor
Calvary Chapel Brighton

CONTENTS

ACKNOWLEDGMENTS

I want to thank the members of the James Gang Home Group and the Band of Brothers Men's Group for all their love and support. I especially want to thank my wife, Marlene, who encouraged me to follow my passion, as well as the many pastors and spiritual teachers who have mentored me over the years.

I want to thank my Lord and Savior for His grace and mercy. I was thirty-nine years old when He lifted the scales from my eyes, allowing me to see the truth. It just goes to show that no matter how young or old you are, God will never give up on you. I am living proof that God will leave the ninety-nine sheep and pursue the one lost sheep. *Thank you, Jesus!*

I do not consider myself a biblical scholar; however, I have tried to capture the insight and wisdom from the many family and friends who have participated in our home groups over the years. Their contribution has been invaluable in putting this study together. My hope is if you are a Christian, this Bible study will reignite your passion for God's Word; and if you are a seeker, my hope and prayer is that God will use this study to woo you into His family. It does not matter how far away you have drifted or what you have done, God loves you and is waiting for you to make a move.

If you are ready to repent and give your life to Jesus, I encourage you to do it now. As the Apostle Paul said to the Corinthians, "*Today is the day of salvation.*" If you are ready to take this step, may I suggest a simple prayer from the Reverend Billy Graham?

> *Dear Lord Jesus, I know that I am a sinner, and I ask for Your forgiveness. I believe You died for my sins and rose from the dead. I turn from my sins and invite You to come into my heart and life. I want to trust and follow You as my Lord and Savior. In Your name. Amen.*

If you have said this prayer and believe it in your heart, may I be the first to welcome you into the family of God. Find yourself a Bible-teaching church and plug in. In time, I hope you'll come to love your new church family as much as I do mine.

INTRODUCTION

This study guide will take you on an exciting adventure with Peter and the rest of the apostles as the Holy Spirit came to live in the heart of believers and empowered ordinary people to change the world through the **Birth of the Church**.

This is a **twelve-week study** and is the first of three studies on the book of Acts.

1. Acts: The Birth of the Church   (12-week study)
2. Acts: Paul's Three Missionary Journeys   (10-week study)
3. Acts: Paul's Arrest, Trial and Imprisonment   (8-week study)

The Purpose of the Church

Jesus established His church to evangelize the world by making disciples and equipping them so they can proclaim the good news to a fallen world through the power of the Holy Spirit.

The Holy Spirit.
You will receive power when the Holy Spirit has come upon you; and you shall be My witnesses both in Jerusalem and in all Judea, and Samaria, and as far as the remotest part of the earth. (Acts 1:8)

Equip the Saints.
He gave some as apostles, some as prophets, some as evangelists, some as pastors and teachers, for the equipping of the saints for the work of ministry, for the building up of the body of Christ. (Ephesians 4:11–12)

All Scripture is inspired by God and beneficial for teaching, for rebuke, for correction, for training in righteousness; so that the man or woman of God may be fully capable, equipped for every good work. (2 Timothy 3:16–17)

Build up the Saints.
Therefore, encourage one another and build one another up, just as you also are doing. (1 Thessalonians 5:11)

Encourage one another in love and good deeds, not abandoning our own meeting together, as is the habit of some people, but encouraging one another; and all the more as you see the day drawing near. (Hebrews 10:24–25)

Fellowship.

They were continually devoting themselves to the apostles' teaching and to fellowship, to the breaking of bread and to prayer. (Acts 2:42)

I am giving you a new commandment, that you love one another; just as I have loved you, that you also love one another. (John 13:34)

Preach the Gospel and Make Disciples.

Jesus came up and spoke to them, saying, "Go, therefore, and make disciples of all the nations, baptizing them in the name of the Father and the Son and the Holy Spirit, teaching them to follow all that I commanded you; and behold, I am with you always, to the end of the age. (Matthew 28:18–20)

How to Use This Study

This study guide is set up for 8–12 people and each weekly study should take approximately 60–70 minutes to complete. There are two sections in the study. The odd-numbered pages are the study guide, and the even-numbered pages contain the answers to the study guide questions. Therefore, you don't need to be an expert on the Bible to facilitate a group, you just need to have a desire and a willingness to draw closer to God and to other believers.

The study is arranged so that everyone has the opportunity to participate by reading a section and then answering the questions from that section. The end of each section is marked by a solid black line that says

STOP AND DISCUSS THE ABOVE

At this point, the reader can choose to answer the questions or pass. After the reader has answered the questions or passed, the discussion is then opened up to the group. Once the group discussion for that section has been completed, the facilitator or reader should read the answers on the back of the page.

Then the next person reads the ensuing section. This continues in round-robin style, until the entire study has been read. The end of the study is designated with **"Let's RE-Read Tonight's Verses."**

In this section, each person reads to the ~~~~ separator and then rotates readers until the entire chapter has been read. This is a very important step and should not be skipped. It is amazing how the Holy Spirit will bring a new level of understanding after the entire chapter has been studied verse by verse and then reread in its entirety.

Group Guidelines

1. Silence all cell phones.
2. Stay focused and set aside outside factors.
3. Give the group your full attention.
4. Encourage everyone to participate and to ask questions.
5. No one person should dominate the discussion; everyone's input matters.
6. Confidentiality is a must. What said in the group, stays in the group.
7. Each group should start and end with prayer.
8. Have fun!

A Precept Bible Study

ACTS

The Birth of the Church

Week 1, Acts 1:1–26

A Verse-by-Verse Journey through the book of Acts

The book of Acts was written by Luke and his attention to detail provides us a unique look into the birth of the church and the struggles the early church faced.

What do we know about the book of Acts?

- Author: Luke
- Written to: Theophilus
- When: approximately AD 62.

What do we know about the author, Luke?

- He was a doctor who wrote the **Gospel of Luke** and was the only Gentile author in the New Testament (Colossians 4:11–14).
- He was known as *Luke the Evangelist.*
- He was not an eyewitness to Jesus's ministry (Luke 1:1–4).
- He traveled with the Apostle Paul and wrote this letter to describe the birth of the church and Paul's three missionary journeys.
- He died at the age of eighty-four in Boeotia.

This study is on the first twelve chapters from the book of Acts and is reflected in the chart below. The chart also gives us a glimpse into the rest of Acts, as the church expanded throughout the Mediterranean region.

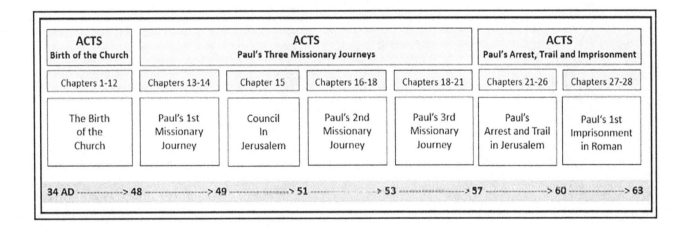

ACTS Birth of the Church	ACTS Paul's Three Missionary Journeys				ACTS Paul's Arrest, Trail and Imprisonment	
Chapters 1-12	Chapters 13-14	Chapter 15	Chapters 16-18	Chapters 18-21	Chapters 21-26	Chapters 27-28
The Birth of the Church	Paul's 1st Missionary Journey	Council In Jerusalem	Paul's 2nd Missionary Journey	Paul's 3rd Missionary Journey	Paul's Arrest and Trail in Jerusalem	Paul's 1st Imprisonment in Roman

34 AD --------> 48 --------> 49 --------> 51 --------> 53 --------> 57 --------> 60 --------> 63

(Q) Any More Comments?_____

Stop and Discuss the Above Comments.

Let's Begin Tonight's Study

> **Acts 1:1–2a (NASB).** [1] **The first account** I **composed, [to] Theophilus**, about all that Jesus began to do and teach, [2] until the day when He was taken up to heaven, after He had by the Holy Spirit given orders to the apostles whom He had chosen.

Commentary. In verse 1, Luke told us that he was the author of the book of Acts and that his previous letter, that he referred to as his *"first account,"* was written to *"tell people all about what Jesus did and what Jesus taught."* He also told us that both of his letters were written to Theophilus.

(Q) WHAT IS THE *"first account"* MENTIONED IN VERSE 1? (Read Luke 1:3–4.)

_____

(Q) WHO IS THEOPHILUS?_____

(Q) ANY COMMENTS ON THESE VERSES?_____

STOP AND DISCUSS THE ABOVE VERSES AND QUESTIONS. Answers to questions are on the next page.

> **Acts 1:3 (NASB).** [3] To these **He also presented Himself alive** after His suffering, by many convincing proofs, appearing to them over a period of **forty days** and speaking of the things concerning the kingdom of God.

Commentary. After the resurrection, Jesus appeared to the apostles and to more than five hundred men and women for forty days. During this forty-day period, Jesus was giving a masters level course on *"the things concerning the kingdom of God."*

(Q) WHY WAS IT NECESSARY FOR JESUS TO APPEAR TO THE DISCIPLES AFTER THIS RESURRECTION?

_____

(Q) ANY COMMENTS ON THESE VERSES?_____

STOP AND DISCUSS THE ABOVE VERSES AND QUESTIONS. Answers to questions are on the next page.

ANSWERS TO QUESTIONS FROM THE PREVIOUS PAGE

(Q) WHAT IS THE *"first account"* MENTIONED IN VERSE 1?

- Luke is referring to the **Gospel of Luke** that he wrote to **Theophilus**.

   It seemed fitting to me as well, having investigated everything carefully from the beginning, to write it out for you in an orderly sequence, most excellent Theophilus; so that you may know the exact truth about the things you have been taught. (Luke 1:3–4)

(Q) WHO IS THEOPHILUS?

No one knows the true identity of Theophilus. However, there are several theories about who he was:

1. Theophilus was an honorary title and not a person; therefore, Luke's letter was addressed to anyone who had that title.
2. Some believe Theophilus may have been Paul's lawyer during his trial in Rome.
3. Some believe the letter was addressed to Theophilus ben Ananus, the high priest in Jerusalem from AD 37 to AD 41. That would make him the son of Annas and brother-in-law of Caiaphas.
4. The most likely possibility is that Theophilus was a person of honor since Luke referred to him as "most excellent Theophilus." Many scholars believe he may have been wealthy and helped support Paul during his missionary journeys, and Luke was giving him a detailed report on his journeys.

(Q) WHY WAS IT NECESSARY FOR JESUS TO APPEAR TO THE DISCIPLES AFTER HIS RESURRECTION?

- To continue discipling and teaching.
- To tell the apostles to stay in Jerusalem and wait for the Holy Spirit to come.
- To show the apostles and everyone else that He was alive.
- Christianity is based on the resurrection. If Jesus hadn't risen from the dead, the Bible says that His followers should be pitied for believing in a dead man (1 Corinthians 15:17).

> **Acts 1:4–5 (NASB).** ⁴Gathering them together, He commanded them not to leave Jerusalem, but to **wait for what the Father had promised**,
>
> "*Which,*" He said, "*you heard from Me; ⁵ for John baptized with water, but you will be baptized with the Holy Spirit not many days from now.*"

Commentary. Obviously, verse 5 referred to John the Baptist or, as some call him, John the Baptizer. John was prophesized in Isaiah as the "*lone voice crying out in the wilderness*" for declaring the coming of the Messiah.

(Q) What Was the Promise Mentioned in These Verses?_____

(Q) Any Comments on These Verses?_____

STOP AND DISCUSS THE ABOVE VERSES AND QUESTIONS. Answers to questions are on the next page.

> **Acts 1:6–8a (NASB).** ⁶So when they had come together, they were asking Him, saying,
>
> "*Lord, is it at this time You are restoring the kingdom to Israel?*"
>
> ⁷He said to them,
>
> "*It is not for you to know times or epochs which the Father has fixed by His own authority; ⁸ but you will receive power when the Holy Spirit has come upon you.*"

Commentary. Some Jews were hoping that when the Messiah returned, He would come as an earthly conqueror and free Israel from Roman control. As we know, the kingdom Jesus spoke of was a **spiritual kingdom** that He would establish in the hearts and lives of believers, in the person of the Holy Spirit.

(Q) According to These Verses, When Is Jesus Going to Return and Restore His Kingdom?

_____

(Q) Any Comments on These Verses?_____

STOP AND DISCUSS THE ABOVE VERSES AND QUESTIONS. Answers to questions are on the next page.

Answers to Questions from the Previous Page

(Q) What Was the Promise Mentioned in These Verses?

- The Holy Spirit is going to come.
- *"You will be baptized with the **Holy Spirit**"* (Acts 1:5).
- *"You will receive **power** when the Holy Spirit has come upon you"* (Acts 1:8).

(Q) According to These Verses, When Is Jesus Going to Return and Restore His Kingdom?

- *"It is not for you to know times or epochs which the Father has fixed by His own authority"* (Acts 1:7a).
- In other words, no one knows when Jesus will return.
- Do not pay attention to anyone who claims they know when Jesus will return because they are a false teacher.

> **Acts 1:8a (NASB).** [8] *"You will receive power when the Holy Spirit has come upon you."*

Commentary. When a person gives their life to Jesus, the Holy Spirit takes up permanent residence in the body of the believer (John 14:17). The Holy Spirit is evidence that the person has been adopted into the family of God and been sealed for the day of redemption (Ephesians 1:13–14). What an awesome promise from God that as believers, we can experience the power of the Holy Spirit in our lives.

(Q) WHAT IS THE PURPOSE OF THE HOLY SPIRIT AND WHAT ARE HIS CHARACTERISTICS?

_____

Read Acts 1:8, John 14:16–17, John 14:26, John 16:13–14, Romans 8:26, Romans 15:13, Ephesians 3:16, Luke 12:12, Isaiah 11:2, 2 Corinthians 3:17, 2 Timothy 1:7, Titus 3:5

(Q) ANY COMMENTS ON THESE VERSES?_____

STOP AND DISCUSS THE ABOVE VERSES AND QUESTIONS. Answers to questions are on the next page.

> **Acts 1:8b (NASB).** [8] *"And you shall be My witnesses both in Jerusalem, and in all Judea and Samaria, and even to the remotest part of the earth."*

Commentary. Verse 8 refers to the *Great Commission* which Jesus commanded in the Gospel of Matthew.

> *Go therefore and make disciples of all the nations, baptizing them in the name of the Father and the Son and the Holy Spirit, teaching them to observe all that I commanded you; and lo, I am with you always, even to the end of the age. (Matthew 28:19–20)*

The book of Acts can be described as the Great Commission in action. In this study, we will follow the apostles as they share the good news of salvation and teach others all that Jesus taught them.

(Q) WHAT DOES *Judea and Samaria* REPRESENT?_____

(Q) ANY COMMENTS ON THESE VERSES?_____

STOP AND DISCUSS THE ABOVE VERSES AND QUESTIONS. Answers to questions are on the next page.

(Q) WHAT IS THE PURPOSE OF THE HOLY SPIRIT AND WHAT ARE HIS CHARACTERISTICS?

Power	Guidance	Inner strength	Freedom
Helper	Intercede on our behalf	Self-control	Regeneration
Teacher	Gives us words to say	Hope	Wisdom
Seal	Conviction	Discernment	

References: Acts 1:8, John 14:16–17, John 14:26, John 16:13–14, Romans 8:26, Romans 15:13, Ephesians 3:16, Luke 12:12, Isaiah 11:2, 2 Corinthians 3:17, 2 Timothy 1:7, Titus 3:5.

(Q) WHAT DOES *Judea and Samaria* REPRESENT?

- **Judea** is the southern kingdom of Israel and means *Land of the Jews.*
- **Samaria** is the northern kingdom of Israel.
- Therefore, Judea and Samaria represent ***all of Israel.***

> **Acts 1:9–11 (NASB).** [9] And after He had said these things, He was lifted up while they were looking on, and a cloud received Him out of their sight. [10] And as they were gazing intently into the sky while He was going, behold, two men in white clothing stood beside them. [11] They also said,
> *"Men of Galilee, why do you stand looking into the sky? This Jesus, who has been taken up from you into heaven, will come in just the same way as you have watched Him go into heaven."*

Commentary. The two men in white clothing had a message for the disciples. The message was that Jesus will return in the same way as He left; suddenly, in a body and visible to all. In 1 Thessalonians, Paul wrote *"the day of the Lord will come like a thief in the night."*

To illustrate this point, Jesus told a parable about ten bridesmaids who were awaiting a bridegroom. Five prepared, and five did not. The five bridesmaids who prepared were wise and brought oil for their lamps while the other five bridesmaids were foolish and did not bring oil for their lamps. When they went to buy oil, the bridegroom came, and they were left behind (Matthew 25:1–13).

OUR LESSON: We should be vigilant and ready for Jesus's return at all times.

(Q) WHO WERE THE TWO MEN DRESSED IN WHITE CLOTHING?_____

(Q) HOW CAN A NONBELIEVER "GET READY" FOR JESUS'S RETURN?_____

(Q) ANY COMMENTS ON THESE VERSES?_____

STOP AND DISCUSS THE ABOVE VERSES AND QUESTIONS. Answers to questions are on the next page.

> **Acts 1:12 (NASB).** [12] Then they returned to Jerusalem from the mount called Olivet, which is near Jerusalem, a **Sabbath day's journey** away.

Commentary. The Bible recorded many significant events that occurred at the Mount of Olives. Maybe the most known event was the night Judas betrayed Jesus and led a group of soldiers to the Garden of Gethsemane on the Mount of Olives, which was just outside of Jerusalem.

The apostles obeyed Jesus's command to go back to Jerusalem and wait for the Holy Spirit to come. Jerusalem was only a Sabbath day's journey away from Mount Olivet.

(Q) HOW LONG IS A SABBATH DAY'S JOURNEY?_____

(Q) ANY COMMENTS ON THESE VERSES?_____

STOP AND DISCUSS THE ABOVE VERSES AND QUESTIONS. Answers to questions are on the next page.

Answers to Questions from the Previous Page

(Q) Who Were the Two Men Dressed in White Clothing?

- They were angels.

(Q) How Can a Nonbeliever "Get Ready" for Jesus's Return?

- Admit you are sinner and repent.
- Ask Jesus to be your Lord.
- Confess your sins and ask for forgiveness.
- Get a Bible and commit to reading it consistently.
- Commit to praying daily.
- Find a home church and attend it regularly.
- Fellowship with other believers and don't go to slippery places.

If you are ready to take this step, may I suggest a simple prayer from the Reverend Billy Graham?

Dear Lord Jesus, I know that I am a sinner, and I ask for Your forgiveness. I believe You died for my sins and rose from the dead. I turn from my sins and invite You to come into my heart and life. I want to trust and follow You as my Lord and Savior. In Your name. Amen.

If you have said this prayer and it expresses the desire of your heart, welcome to the family of God.

(Q) How Long Is a Sabbath Day's Journey?

- It is the distance a Jew was allowed to travel on the Sabbath without breaking **the Law**.
- The limit was two thousand cubits.
- This would make the distance of the Sabbath day's journey about **1,000–1,200 yards**.

> **Acts 1:13–14 (NASB).** ¹³ When they had entered the city, **they went up to the upper room** where they were staying; that is, Peter and John and James and Andrew, Philip and Thomas, Bartholomew and Matthew, James the son of Alphaeus, and Simon the Zealot, and Judas the son of James.
> ¹⁴ **These all with one mind were continually devoting themselves to pray**er, along with the women, and Mary the mother of Jesus, and with His brothers.

Commentary. In these verses, the apostles demonstrated several things that we should imitate:

- They obeyed God.
- They devoted themselves to prayer (they prayed without ceasing).
- They were committed to each other (one mind).

(Q) WHO WERE JESUS'S BROTHERS MENTIONED IN VERSE 14b? (Read Matthew 1:55)

_____

(Q) ANY COMMENTS ON THESE VERSES?_____

REFLECTIVE QUESTION: How is my prayer life? Do I make time for God, or am I too busy?

STOP AND DISCUSS THE ABOVE VERSES AND QUESTIONS. Answers to questions are on the next page.

> **Acts 1:15–17 (NASB).** ¹⁵ At this time, Peter stood up in the midst of the brethren (a gathering of about **one hundred and twenty persons** was there together), and said,
> ¹⁶ *"Brethren, the Scripture had to be fulfilled, which the Holy Spirit foretold by the mouth of David concerning Judas, who became a guide to those who arrested Jesus. ¹⁷ For he was counted among us and received his share in this ministry."*

Commentary. There were 120 family and friends of the apostles who followed Jesus for the three and a half years of His ministry. The 120 people can be categorized into four groups according to who was **closest to Jesus:**

1. Peter, John, and James
2. The remaining apostles
3. Mary, Martha, Mary
4. The 120 family and friends

Peter stood up to remind the believers that Judas's betrayal of Jesus was foretold by David in Psalm 55 and fulfilled the scripture's prophecy.

(Q) WHAT DO WE KNOW ABOUT JUDAS?_____

(Q) ANY COMMENTS ON THESE VERSES?_____

STOP AND DISCUSS THE ABOVE VERSES AND QUESTIONS. Answers to questions are on the next page.

(Q) Who Were Jesus's Brothers Mentioned in Verse 14b?

- Mary and Joseph had four boys and an unknown number of daughters. Therefore, Jesus had four brothers and more than one sister. The Gospel's of Matthew and Mark both confirm Jesus's siblings.

  Is this not the carpenter's son? Is His mother not called Mary, and His brothers, James, Joseph, Simon, and Judas, and his sisters? (Matthew 13:55)

  Is this not the carpenter, the son of Mary and brother of James, Joseph, Judas, and Simon? (Mark 6:3)

(Q) What Do We Know about Judas?

- He was chosen by Jesus to be one of the twelve apostles (John 6:70).
- He served as the treasurer for the apostles and kept the money bag (John 12:6).
- He was greedy (John 12:6).
- He betrayed Jesus for thirty pieces of silver (Luke 22:3–4).
- After he betrayed Jesus, Satan entered him (John 13:27).
- He committed suicide instead of seeking forgiveness (Matthew 27:5).
- Judas fulfilled the Old Testament prophecy that he would betray Jesus (Psalm 41:9).

> **Acts 1:18a (NASB).** ¹⁸ Now this man [Judas] acquired a field with the price of his wickedness.

Commentary. Verse 18 says that Judas *"acquired a field,"* but this seems to contradict Matthew's account which says the chief priest bought the field.

Matthew's account.

> And [Judas] threw the pieces of silver into the temple sanctuary and left; and he went away and hanged himself. The chief priests took the pieces of silver and said, "It is not lawful to put them in the temple treasury, since it is money paid for blood." And [the chief priests] conferred together and with the money bought the Potter's Field as a burial place for strangers. For this reason that field has been called the Field of Blood to this day. (Matthew 27:5–8)

(Q) DOES LUKE'S ACCOUNT CONTRADICT MATTHEW'S ACCOUNT ON WHO BOUGHT THE FIELD? WHY OR WHY NOT?_____

(Q) ANY COMMENTS ON THESE VERSES?_____

STOP AND DISCUSS THE ABOVE VERSES AND QUESTIONS. Answers to questions are on the next page.

> **Acts 1:18b–19 (NASB).** ¹⁸ And **falling headlong, he burst open in the middle and all his intestines gushed out.** ¹⁹ And it became known to all who were living in Jerusalem; so that in their own language that field was called Hakeldama, that is, Field of Blood.

Commentary. Verses 18b–19 describe Judas's death as *"falling headlong and his intestines gushed out."* Once again, Luke's account seems to contradict Matthew's account which says Judas hung himself.

Matthew's account.

> And he [Judas] went away and hanged himself. (Matthew 27:5b)

(Q) DOES LUKE'S ACCOUNT CONTRADICT MATTHEW'S ACCOUNT ON HOW JUDAS DIED? WHY OR WHY NOT?

_____

(Q) ANY COMMENTS ON THESE VERSES?_____

STOP AND DISCUSS THE ABOVE VERSES AND QUESTIONS. Answers to questions are on the next page.

ANSWERS TO QUESTIONS FROM THE PREVIOUS PAGE

(Q) DOES LUKE'S ACCOUNT CONTRADICT MATTHEW'S ACCOUNT ON WHO BOUGHT THE FIELD?

- Acts 1:18 says **Judas** was the man who *"bought a field."*
- Matthew 27:6–7 says the **chief priests** were the *true purchasers of the field.*

Explanation: Since the chief priests used the thirty pieces of silver from Judas, the field was **indirectly purchased by Judas**. Therefore, there is no contradiction.

(Q) DOES LUKE'S ACCOUNT CONTRADICT MATTHEW'S ACCOUNT ON HOW JUDAS DIED?

- Judas hung himself (Matthew 27:5b).
- He was left to hang there long enough to **decompose**, and then he fell to the ground, thereby causing the eruption of all his bowels (Acts 1:18b–19).

Explanation: The two events occurred in sequence. First, Judas hung himself and was left hanging on the tree until the body decomposed. Then he fell to the ground and his bowels erupted. Therefore, there is no contradiction.

Acts 1:20–26 (NASB). ²⁰ *"For it is written in the book of Psalms,*

'LET HIS HOMESTEAD BE MADE DESOLATE,   ← *Psalm 69:25*
AND LET NO ONE DWELL IN IT'; and
'LET ANOTHER MAN TAKE HIS OFFICE.'   ← *Psalm 109:8*

²¹ *Therefore it is necessary that of the men who have accompanied us all the time that the Lord Jesus went in and out among us—*²² *beginning with the baptism of John until the day that He was taken up from us, one of these must become a witness with us of His resurrection."*

²³ So they put forward two men, Joseph called Barsabbas (who was also called Justus), and Matthias. ²⁴ And **they prayed and said,**

"You, Lord, who know the hearts of all people, show which one of these two You have chosen ²⁵ *to occupy this ministry and apostleship from which Judas turned aside to go to his own place."*

²⁶ And **they drew lots for them, and the lot fell to Matthias; and he was added to the eleven apostles.**

Commentary. Peter quoted the Old Testament, where the psalmist said, *"LET ANOTHER MAN TAKE HIS OFFICE."* Peter used these verses as a reason to replace Judas.

Then in verse 21, Peter listed the requirements for selecting a replacement for Judas as an apostle:
- The man had to have been with them the entire time of Jesus's ministry, and
- The man had to have been a witness of the resurrection and ascension of Jesus.

Was Matthias the Lord's choice to replace Judas?

Some people have suggested the Apostle Paul, not Matthias, was God's choice for the twelfth apostle. They argue that Jesus told the apostles to wait for the coming of the Holy Spirit and that casting lots is not how the apostles should have made the decision.

(Q) WHAT ARE YOUR THOUGHTS ON WHO SHOULD HAVE REPLACED JUDAS (MATTHIAS OR PAUL)?
_____

(Q) ANY COMMENTS ON THESE VERSES?_____

STOP AND DISCUSS THE ABOVE VERSES AND QUESTIONS. **Answers to questions are on the next page.**

ANSWERS TO QUESTIONS FROM THE PREVIOUS PAGE

(Q) WHAT ARE YOUR THOUGHTS ON WHO SHOULD HAVE REPLACED JUDAS (MATTHIAS OR PAUL)?

- The New Testament does not condone or condemn the way the apostles made the decision.
- Casting lots was an acceptable method for making a decision in ancient Israel.
- In verses 24 and 25, the apostles prayed and asked God to choose Judas's replacement.
- Paul would not have been qualified based on the apostles' criteria.
- So who's name will be written on the **twelfth throne** in the heavenly Jerusalem?

  And Jesus said to them, "Truly I say to you, that you who have followed Me, in the regeneration when the Son of Man will sit on His glorious throne, you also shall sit upon twelve thrones, judging the twelve tribes of Israel." (Matthew 19:28)

- The Bible does not explicitly say, but it likely will be **Matthias**.
- However, in the end, we will have to wait until we get to heaven to find out.

Let's RE-Read Tonight's Verses

Acts 1:1–26 (NASB). [1] The first account I composed, Theophilus, about all that Jesus began to do and teach, [2] until the day when He was taken up to heaven, after He had given orders by the Holy Spirit to the apostles whom He had chosen.

----

[3] To these He also presented Himself alive after His suffering, by many convincing proofs, appearing to them over a period of forty days and speaking of things regarding the kingdom of God.

----

[4] Gathering them together, He commanded them not to leave Jerusalem, but to wait for what the Father had promised,
> *"Which," He said, "you heard of from Me;* [5] *for John baptized with water, but you will be baptized with the Holy Spirit not many days from now."*

----

[6] So, when they had come together, they began asking Him, saying,
> *"Lord, is it at this time that You are restoring the kingdom to Israel?"*

----

[7] But He said to them,
> *"It is not for you to know periods of time or appointed times which the Father has set by His own authority;* [8] *but you will receive power when the Holy Spirit has come upon you; and you shall be My witnesses both in Jerusalem and in all Judea, and Samaria, and as far as the remotest part of the earth."*

----

[9] And after He had said these things, He was lifted up while they were watching, and a cloud took Him up, out of their sight.

----

[10] And as they were gazing intently into the sky while He was going, then behold, two men in white clothing stood beside them, [11] and they said,
> *"Men of Galilee, why do you stand looking into the sky? This Jesus, who has been taken up from you into heaven, will come in the same way as you have watched Him go into heaven."*

----

[12] Then they returned to Jerusalem from the mountain called Olivet, which is near Jerusalem, a Sabbath day's journey away. [13] When they had entered the city, they went up to the upstairs room where they were staying, that is, Peter, John, James, and Andrew, Philip and Thomas, Bartholomew and Matthew, James the son of Alphaeus, Simon the Zealot, and Judas the son of James.

----

[14] All these were continually devoting themselves with one mind to prayer, along with the women, and Mary the mother of Jesus, and with His brothers.

----

¹⁵ At this time Peter stood up among the brothers and sisters (a group of about 120 people was there together), and said,

> ¹⁶ *"Brothers, the Scripture had to be fulfilled, which the Holy Spirit foretold by the mouth of David concerning Judas, who became a guide to those who arrested Jesus. ¹⁷ For he was counted among us and received his share in this ministry."*

~~~~~~

¹⁸ (Now this man acquired a field with the price of his wickedness, and falling headlong, he burst open in the middle and all his intestines gushed out. ¹⁹ And it became known to all the residents of Jerusalem; as a result that field was called Hakeldama in their own language, that is, Field of Blood.)

~~~~~~

> ²⁰ *"For it is written in the book of Psalms:*
> *'MAY HIS RESIDENCE BE MADE DESOLATE, AND MAY THERE BE NONE LIVING IN IT';*
> *and, 'MAY ANOTHER TAKE HIS OFFICE.'"*

~~~~~~

> ²¹ *"Therefore it is necessary that of the men who have accompanied us all the time that the Lord Jesus went in and out among us—²² beginning with the baptism of John until the day that He was taken up from us—one of these must become a witness with us of His resurrection."*

~~~~~~

²³ So they put forward two men, Joseph called Barsabbas (who was also called Justus), and Matthias. ²⁴ And they prayed and said,

> *"You, Lord, who know the hearts of all people, show which one of these two You have chosen ²⁵ to occupy this ministry and apostleship from which Judas turned aside to go to his own place."*

~~~~~~

²⁶ And they drew lots for them, and the lot fell to Matthias; and he was added to the eleven apostles.

(Q) ANY FINAL COMMENTS?_____

THIS IS THE END OF THIS WEEK'S STUDY.

A Precept Bible Study

ACTS

The Birth of the Church

Week 2, Acts 2:1–47

A Verse-by-Verse Journey through the book of Acts

Let's Review Last Week's Study

The book of Acts was written by Luke to Theophilus after the death and resurrection of Jesus and documents the birth of the Christian church, as well as the three missionary journeys by the Apostle Paul.

In chapter 1, Luke reminded us that after the resurrection, Jesus appeared to over five hundred people and that Jesus gave His followers a commandment to stay in Jerusalem to wait for the Holy Spirit to come. After forty days, Jesus ascended into heaven, and then two angels appeared and told the apostles that when Jesus returns, He will come the same way He left: suddenly, from the sky, and visible to all.

Chapter 1 ended with the eleven apostles appointing Matthias to replace Judas as the twelfth apostle.

(Q) ANY OTHER COMMENTS ON CHAPTER 1?_____

STOP AND DISCUSS THE ABOVE COMMENTS.

Let's Review Tonight's Study

Chapter 2 begins with the apostles gathered together for the Pentecost celebration. As we know, **Passover and Pentecost** have different meanings for the Jews than they do for Christians.

PASSOVER

JEWS	CHRISTIANS
• Also known as the Feast of the Unleavened Bread. • God sent 10 plagues over Egypt. • God told the Jews to spread blood/lamb over their doorways so the **angel of death will pass over them**. • Pharaoh let Moses and the Israelites go.	• Christians celebrate the death and resurrection of Jesus, commonly referred to as **Easter**. • Jesus is the Lamb of God who takes away the sins of the world.

PENTECOST

JEWS	CHRISTIANS
• Pentecost is celebrated 50 days after Passover. • Pentecost is the celebration of the completion of the Spring Harvest season. • During Pentecost, Jews offer *two leavened loaves of bread* and *sacrifice two lambs* as a thanks offering to God. • God gave Moses the Ten Commandments on Mount Sinai.	• Christians celebrate Pentecost as the day the **Holy Spirit** descended upon the apostles. • Peter preached in Jerusalem, and 3,000 people committed their lives to Christ. • This is commonly referred to as the birth of the Christian Church.

(Q) ANY COMMENTS ABOUT PASSOVER OR PENTECOST?_____

STOP AND DISCUSS THE ABOVE COMMENTS.

Let's Begin Tonight's Study

> **Acts 2:1–4 (NASB).** [1] When the day of **Pentecost** had come, they were all together in one place. [2] And suddenly there came from heaven a noise like a violent rushing wind, and it filled the whole house where they were sitting. [3] And there appeared to them tongues as of fire distributing themselves, and they rested on each one of them. [4] And they were all filled with the **Holy Spirit** and began to speak with other tongues, as the Spirit was giving them utterance.

Commentary. God chose Pentecost to send His Holy Spirit because He knew the city would be full of people from many nations celebrating Pentecost and this would result in a harvest of new believers. Verse 3 described the Holy Spirit visibly coming upon the apostles as *"tongues of fire,"* enabling them *"to speak with other tongues."*

Some people think that Luke was describing the gift of tongues, but realistically, he was describing the apostles speaking in foreign languages so that all the foreigners attending the Pentecost celebration would understand God's Word in their own language.

(Q) WHAT IS THE *Gift of Tongues,* AND IS IT STILL APPLICABLE TODAY?_____

(Q) ANY OTHER COMMENTS ON THESE VERSES?_____

STOP AND DISCUSS THE ABOVE VERSES AND QUESTIONS. Answers to questions are on the next page.

> **Acts 2:5–13 (NASB).** [5] Now there were Jews living in Jerusalem, devout men from every nation under heaven. [6] And when this sound occurred, the crowd came together, and were bewildered because each one of them was hearing them speak in his own language. [7] They were amazed and astonished, saying,
>> *"Why, are not all these who are speaking Galileans? [8] And how is it that we each hear them in our own language to which we were born? [9] Parthians and Medes and Elamites, and residents of Mesopotamia, Judea and Cappadocia, Pontus and Asia, [10] Phrygia and Pamphylia, Egypt and the districts of Libya around Cyrene, and visitors from Rome, both Jews and proselytes, [11] Cretans and Arabs—we hear them in our own tongues speaking of the mighty deeds of God."*
>
> [12] And they all continued in amazement and great perplexity, saying to one another,
>> *"What does this mean?"*
>
> [13] But **others were mocking** and saying, *"They are full of sweet wine."*

Commentary. Isn't it like people to **mock** others for what they do not understand? *It is still like that today*! Nonbelievers will try and make sense of God from an earthly perspective.

(Q) WHY WOULD SOME NONBELIEVERS MOCK CHRISTIANS?_____

(Q) HOW CAN BELIEVERS CHANGE THE PERCEPTION OF CHRISTIANS?_____

(Q) ANY OTHER COMMENTS ON THESE VERSES?_____

STOP AND DISCUSS THE ABOVE VERSES AND QUESTIONS. Answers to questions are on the next page.

(Q) WHAT IS THE *Gift of Tongues*, AND IS IT STILL APPLICABLE TODAY?

- Speaking in tongues is one of the gifts of the Holy Spirit and is a form of communication to God.
- The other gifts are wisdom, knowledge, faith, healing, miracles, prophecy, discerning spirits, interpreting tongues, administration, and the gift of helps.
- Not everyone can speak in tongues because not everyone is given the gift.
- According to Paul, when someone speaks in tongues, there must be an interpreter.

*Now there are varieties of gifts…to each one is given the manifestation of the Spirit for the common good …[to one is given] various kinds of **tongues, and to another the interpretation of tongues**. (1 Corinthians 12:4,7,10b)*

(Q) WHY DO NONBELIEVERS MOCK CHRISTIANS?

- They say, Christians are known for what they are against, rather than for their *"love."*
- They say, Christians believe in a fantasy world and a make-believe God.
- They say, Christians are rigid and have not changed with the times (not accepting of gay marriage or abortion).
- They say, Christians are hypocrites.

(Q) HOW CAN BELIEVERS CHANGE THE PERCEPTION OF CHRISTIANS?

- In a fallen world, believers may not be able to change this perception.
- Believers can share their testimony to show they are sinners in need of a savior.
- Believers can share the good news that Jesus paid their sin-debt.
- Believers can affirm God's love for everyone as Paul said in his first letter to the Corinthians.

All that you do must be done in love. (1 Corinthians 16:14)

- Believers can affirm their love for others and build relationships.
- Believers can pray for nonbelievers.

> **Acts 2:14–15 (NASB).** ¹⁴ But Peter, taking his stand with the eleven, raised his voice and declared to them:
>
> *"Men of Judea and all you who live in Jerusalem, let this be known to you and give heed to my words. ¹⁵ For these men are not drunk, as you suppose, for it is only the third hour of the day."*

Commentary. Peter defended the apostles by boldly proclaiming to over three thousand people that the apostles were not drunk.

(Q) What Time Is the "*third hour of the day*"?_____

(Q) Any Other Comments on These Verses?_____

Stop and Discuss the Above Verses and Questions. Answers to questions are on the next page.

> **Acts 2:16–24 (NASB).** ¹⁶ *"But this is what was spoken of through the **prophet Joel**:*
> ¹⁷ 'And It Shall Be In the Last Days,'   ← **Joel 2:28–32**
>
> **God says,**
> 'That I Will Pour Forth of My Spirit on All Mankind;
> And Your Sons and Your Daughters Shall Prophesy,
> And Your Young Men Shall See Visions,
> And Your Old Men Shall Dream Dreams;
> ¹⁸ Even on My Bondslaves, Both Men and Women,
> I Will in Those Days Pour Forth of My Spirit.'
> And they shall prophesy.
> ¹⁹ 'And I Will Grant Wonders in the Sky Above
> And Signs on the Earth Below, Blood, and fire, and Vapor of Smoke.
> ²⁰ The Sun Will Be Turned into Darkness And the Moon into Blood,
> Before the Great and Glorious Day of the Lord Shall Come.
> ²¹ And It Shall Be That Everyone Who Calls on the Name of the Lord Will Be
> Saved.'
> ²² *Men of Israel, listen to these words: **Jesus the Nazarene**, a man attested to you by God with miracles and wonders and signs which God performed through Him in your midst, just as you yourselves know—*²³ *this Man, delivered over by the **predetermined plan** and **foreknowledge of God**, you nailed to a cross by the hands of godless men and put Him to death. *²⁴* But God raised Him up again, putting an end to the agony of death, since it was impossible for Him to be held in its power."*

Commentary. Peter began his sermon by quoting the prophet Joel to prove that Jesus is the Messiah who was prophesized in the Old Testament.

(Q) In Verse 22, What Is The Difference Between a Nazarene and a Nazarite?_____

(Q) Identify All of the Prophecies in These Verses?_____

(Q) Any Other Comments on These Verses?_____

Stop and Discuss the Above Verses and Questions. Answers to questions are on the next page.

ANSWERS TO QUESTIONS FROM THE PREVIOUS PAGE

(Q) WHAT TIME IS THE *"third hour of the day"*?

- In ancient Israel, the day started at sunrise (**6:00 a.m.**). Therefore, the third hour would be **9:00 a.m.** (6:00 a.m. plus three hours).

(Q) IN VERSE 22, WHAT IS THE DIFFERENCE BETWEEN A NAZARENE AND A NAZARITE?

NAZARENE

- The term Nazarene refers to someone who lived in the town of Nazareth.

NAZARITE

- A Nazarite is someone who has taken the **Nazarite vow** and voluntarily dedicated themselves to God (Numbers 6:2).
- The Nazarite shall not have wine and strong drink (Numbers 6:3–7).
- The Nazarite shall not eat anything that is produced by the grapevine (Numbers 6:3–7).
- The Nazarite shall not let a razor touch his head and he shall let the locks of his hair grow long (Numbers 6:5).
- The Nazarite shall not touch or go near a dead body (Numbers 6:6).
- Other Nazarites were: Sampson, Samuel, John the Baptist.

(Q) IDENTIFY ALL OF THE PROPHECIES IN THESE VERSES?

Prophecies that have already happened:

- God will pour out His spirit on mankind.
- The Messiah would perform signs and wonders.
- The Messiah would be nailed to a cross by godless men.
- The Messiah would be raised from the dead.
- The sun will be turned into darkness, and the moon into blood. This occurred while Jesus was hanging on the cross.

Prophecies that have yet to happen:

- Wonders in the sky and signs on the earth below, blood, fire, and vapor of smoke.

Acts 2:25–36 (NASB). 25 *"For David says of Him,*
'I Saw the Lord Always in My Presence;　　　　　　　　*← Psalm 16:8–11*
For He Is at My Right Hand, so That I Will Not Be Shaken.
26 *Therefore My Heart Was Glad and My Tongue Exulted;*
Moreover My Flesh Also Will Live in Hope;
27 *Because You Will Not Abandon My Soul to Hades,*
Nor Allow Your Holy One to Undergo Decay.
28 *You Have Made Known to Me the Ways of Life;*
You Will Make Me Full of Gladness with Your Presence.'
29 *Brothers, I may confidently say to you regarding the patriarch David that he both died and was buried, and his tomb is with us to this day.* 30 *So because he was a prophet and knew that God had sworn to him with an oath to seat one of his descendants on his throne,* 31 *he looked ahead and spoke of the resurrection of the Christ, that He was neither abandoned to* **Hades***, nor did His flesh suffer decay.* 32 *It is this Jesus whom God raised up, a fact to which we are all witnesses.*
33 *Therefore, since He has been exalted at the right hand of God, and has received the promise of the Holy Spirit from the Father, He has poured out this which you both see and hear.* 34 *For it was not David who ascended into heaven, but he himself says:*
'The Lord Said to My Lord,　　　　　　　　　　　*← Psalm 110:1*
Sit at My Right Hand, 35 *Until I Make Your Enemies a Footstool for Your Feet.'*
36 *Therefore let all the house of Israel know for certain that God has made Him both Lord and Christ—this* **Jesus whom you crucified***."*

Commentary. In verse 31, Paul mentioned **Hades**. To help us understand more about Hades, we need to discuss what happens when we die. The moment we die, we face the judgment of God (Hebrews 9:27) and are sent to temporary locations to await Jesus's return. Nonbelievers are sent to **Hades** and believers are sent to **Paradise** (Luke 23:43, 2 Corinthians 12:4, Revelation 1:18, 20:13–14). After Jesus died on the cross, He went to lower parts of the earth for three days and then He took the believers in Paradise to heaven and left the unbelievers in Hades.

At the Second Coming of Jesus, those who are in Hades will be thrown into the **Lake of Fire** (Revelation 20:11–15). These are the final and eternal destinations for all people based entirely on whether or not the person put their faith in Jesus Christ for the forgiveness of their sins.

In verses 25–28, Peter was quoting from Psalm 16:8–11 to show that the Old Testament prophesized the Messiah would come from the bloodline of David (verse 30b) and be crucified by the house of Israel (verse 36). In verse 35, Paul quoted Psalm 110:1, which said God would make Jesus's enemies a footstool for His feet. Biblically speaking, a footstool represents lowliness, meekness, and unimportance.

(Q) What Does *"The Lord Said to My Lord"* Mean?_____

(Q) Any Other Comments on These Verses?_____

Stop and Discuss the Above Verses and Questions. Answers to questions are on the next page.

(Q) WHAT DOES "*THE LORD SAID TO MY LORD*" MEAN?

- The first "*Lord*" refers to God, the Father.
- The second "*Lord*" refers to Jesus, the Christ, who sits at God the Father's right hand.
- Therefore, the verse means, *"GOD THE FATHER SAID TO JESUS."*

> **Acts 2:37–40 (NASB).** [37] Now when they heard this, they were pierced to the heart, and said to Peter and the rest of the apostles, *"Brethren, what shall we do?"*
> [38] Peter said to them,
>> *"Repent, and each of you be baptized in the name of Jesus Christ for the forgiveness of your sins; and you will receive the gift of the Holy Spirit. [39] For the promise is for you and your children and for all who are far off, as many as the Lord our God will call to Himself."*
> [40] And with many other words he solemnly testified and kept on exhorting them, saying,
>> *"Be saved from this perverse generation!"*

Commentary. Luke only recorded some of Peter's sermon. How do we know Luke only recorded some of Peter's sermon? We know because verse 40 says, *"Many other words he solemnly testified."* After Peter's sermon, the people asked, *"What shall we do?"* This is the question we must all ask ourselves. Peter answered them and said, *"Repent and be baptized in the name of Jesus."*

(Q) WHAT DOES REPENT MEAN?_____

(Q) IS BAPTISM A REQUIREMENT FOR SALVATION? WHY OR WHY NOT?_____

(Q) ANY OTHER COMMENTS ON THESE VERSES?_____

STOP AND DISCUSS THE ABOVE VERSES AND QUESTIONS. **Answers to questions are on the next page.**

> **Acts 2:41–47 (NASB).** [41] So then, those who had received his word were baptized; and that day **there were added about three thousand souls.** [42] They were continually devoting themselves to the apostles' teaching and to fellowship, to the breaking of bread and to prayer.
> [43] **Everyone kept feeling a sense of awe**; and many wonders and signs were taking place through the apostles. [44] And all those who had believed were together and had all things in common; [45] **and they began selling their property and possessions and were sharing them with all**, as anyone might have need.
> [46] Day by day continuing with one mind in the temple, and breaking bread from house to house, they were taking their meals together with gladness and sincerity of heart, [47] praising God and having favor with all the people. And the Lord was adding to their number day by day those who were being saved.

Commentary. After Peter finished, about three thousand people gave their lives to Jesus. Most people agree that **this was the birth of the church.** These early Christians felt a sense of awe as they witnessed the birth of the Christian church, and their love was so strong they shared their possessions with each other.

REFLECTIVE QUESTIONS: Have you ever been part of a new church plant or a new ministry? Remember the feeling you had when you finally opened the doors for that first meeting? **That is how these new believers felt as Christianity spread throughout Judea.**

(Q) ANY OTHER COMMENTS ON THESE VERSES?_____

STOP AND DISCUSS THE ABOVE COMMENTS.

(Q) WHAT DOES REPENT MEAN?

- Repent means *to change one's mind.*
- Repentance means *a change of mind that results in a change of action.*

(Q) IS BAPTISM A REQUIREMENT FOR SALVATION? WHY OR WHY NOT?

There are many verses that support both of these stances. Below are the most common arguments for both sides of this much-debated issue.

Yes, baptism is required for salvation.

- This is called "baptismal regeneration" and is the belief that regeneration does not occur until a person is water baptized.

No, baptism is not required for salvation.

- Repentance and faith in Jesus are all that is required for salvation. Adding anything else is a works-based salvation and would make salvation dependent on human effort and negate the reason for Jesus going to the cross.
- Therefore, baptism is encouraged as a public declaration of your faith, but it is not a requirement for salvation.

Acts 2:1–47 (NASB). [1] When the day of Pentecost had come, they were all together in one place. [2] And suddenly a noise like a violent rushing wind came from heaven, and it filled the whole house where they were sitting.

[3] And tongues that looked like fire appeared to them, distributing themselves, and a tongue rested on each one of them. [4] And they were all filled with the Holy Spirit and began to speak with different tongues, as the Spirit was giving them the ability to speak out.

[5] Now there were Jews residing in Jerusalem, devout men from every nation under heaven. [6] And when this sound occurred, the crowd came together and they were bewildered, because each one of them was hearing them speak in his own language.

[7] They were amazed and astonished, saying,

"Why, are not all these who are speaking Galileans? [8] *And how is it that we each hear them in our own language to which we were born?* [9] *Parthians, Medes, and Elamites, and residents of Mesopotamia, Judea, and Cappadocia, Pontus and Asia,* [10] *Phrygia and Pamphylia, Egypt and the parts of Libya around Cyrene, and visitors from Rome, both Jews and proselytes,* [11] *Cretans and Arabs—we hear them speaking in our own tongues of the mighty deeds of God."*

[12] And they all continued in amazement and great perplexity, saying to one another,
"What does this mean?"
[13] But others were jeering and saying,
"They are full of sweet wine!"

[14] But **Peter**, taking his stand with the other eleven, raised his voice and declared to them:
"Men of Judea and all you who live in Jerusalem, know this, and pay attention to my words. [15] *For these people are not drunk, as you assume, since it is only the third hour of the day;"*

[16] "but this is what has been spoken through the prophet Joel:
[17] 'AND IT SHALL BE IN THE LAST DAYS,'
God says,
'THAT I WILL POUR OUT MY SPIRIT ON ALL MANKIND;
AND YOUR SONS AND YOUR DAUGHTERS WILL PROPHESY,
AND YOUR YOUNG MEN WILL SEE VISIONS,
AND YOUR OLD MEN WILL HAVE DREAMS;'"

¹⁸ "'AND EVEN ON MY MALE AND FEMALE SERVANTS
I WILL POUR OUT MY SPIRIT IN THOSE DAYS,
AND THEY WILL PROPHESY.
¹⁹ AND I WILL DISPLAY WONDERS IN THE SKY ABOVE
AND SIGNS ON THE EARTH BELOW,
BLOOD, FIRE, AND VAPOR OF SMOKE.
²⁰ THE SUN WILL BE TURNED INTO DARKNESS
AND THE MOON INTO BLOOD,
BEFORE THE GREAT AND GLORIOUS DAY OF THE LORD COMES.
²¹ AND IT SHALL BE THAT EVERYONE WHO CALLS ON THE NAME OF THE LORD WILL BE SAVED.'"

----

²² "Men of Israel, listen to these words: Jesus the Nazarene, a Man attested to you by God with miracles and wonders and signs which God performed through Him in your midst, just as you yourselves know—²³ this Man, delivered over by the predetermined plan and foreknowledge of God, you nailed to a cross by the hands of godless men and put Him to death."

----

²⁴ "But God raised Him from the dead, putting an end to the agony of death, since it was impossible for Him to be held in its power. ²⁵ For David says of Him,
'I SAW THE LORD CONTINUALLY BEFORE ME,
BECAUSE HE IS AT MY RIGHT HAND, SO THAT I WILL NOT BE SHAKEN.
²⁶ THEREFORE MY HEART WAS GLAD AND MY TONGUE WAS OVERJOYED;
MOREOVER MY FLESH ALSO WILL LIVE IN HOPE;
²⁷ FOR YOU WILL NOT ABANDON MY SOUL TO HADES,
NOR WILL YOU ALLOW YOUR HOLY ONE TO UNDERGO DECAY.
²⁸ YOU HAVE MADE KNOWN TO ME THE WAYS OF LIFE;
YOU WILL MAKE ME FULL OF GLADNESS WITH YOUR PRESENCE.'"

----

²⁹ "Brothers, I may confidently say to you regarding the patriarch David that he both died and was buried, and his tomb is with us to this day. ³⁰ So because he was a prophet and knew that God had sworn to him with an oath to seat one of his descendants on his throne, ³¹ he looked ahead and spoke of the resurrection of the Christ, that He was neither abandoned to Hades, nor did His flesh suffer decay."

----

³² "It is this Jesus whom God raised up, a fact to which we are all witnesses. ³³ Therefore, since He has been exalted at the right hand of God, and has received the promise of the Holy Spirit from the Father, He has poured out this which you both see and hear."

----

34 *"For it was not David who ascended into heaven, but he himself says:*
'The Lord said to my Lord,
Sit at My right hand,
35 *Until I make Your enemies a footstool for Your feet.'*
36 *Therefore let all the house of Israel know for certain that God has made Him both Lord and Christ—this Jesus whom you crucified."*

‑‑‑

37 Now when they heard this, they were pierced to the heart, and said to Peter and the rest of the apostles,
   "Brothers, what are we to do?"
38 Peter said to them,
   "Repent, and each of you be baptized in the name of Jesus Christ for the forgiveness of your sins; and you will receive the gift of the Holy Spirit. 39 *For the promise is for you and your children and for all who are far away, as many as the Lord our God will call to Himself."*

‑‑‑

40 And with many other words he solemnly testified and kept on urging them, saying,
   "Be saved from this perverse generation!"
41 So then, those who had received his word were baptized; and that day there were added about three thousand souls. 42 They were continually devoting themselves to the apostles' teaching and to fellowship, to the breaking of bread and to prayer.

‑‑‑

43 Everyone kept feeling a sense of awe; and many wonders and signs were taking place through the apostles. 44 And all the believers were together and had all things in common; 45 and they would sell their property and possessions and share them with all, to the extent that anyone had need.

‑‑‑

46 Day by day continuing with one mind in the temple, and breaking bread from house to house, they were taking their meals together with gladness and sincerity of heart, 47 praising God and having favor with all the people. And the Lord was adding to their number day by day those who were being saved.

‑‑‑

(Q) Any Final Comments?_____

This is the end of this week's study.

A Precept Bible Study

ACTS

The Birth of the Church

Week 3, Acts 3:1–26

A Verse-by-Verse Journey through the book of Acts

Let's Review the First Two Chapters

- Acts picked up where the Gospels ended and covered the next thirty-two years after the resurrection and ascension of Jesus into heaven.
- Acts was written by Luke to Theophilus.
  - Luke was a doctor and a Gentile.
  - Luke is the only Gentile author in the New Testament and wrote the Gospel of Luke.
  - Luke was known as *Luke the Evangelist.*
  - Luke was not an eyewitness to Jesus's ministry; however, he traveled with the Apostle Paul and wrote about what happened during Paul's three missionary journeys.
  - Luke died at the age of eighty-four years.
- Acts described how the apostles demonstrated their faith:
  - They obeyed God.
  - They were devoted to prayer.
  - They were committed to each other and shared their possessions.
- Acts mentioned that Jesus had four brothers: James, Joseph, Simon, and Judas.
- Acts mentioned there were 120 people who followed Jesus throughout His ministry.
- We learned the definition of a Sabbath day's journey.
- We discussed the *job description* of the Holy Spirit.
- Acts described *how* and *why* the apostles chose Matthias to replace Judas as the twelfth apostle.
- We discussed Passover and Pentecost and used them to compare the Jewish beliefs to the Christian beliefs.
- We discussed the *gifts of the Spirit*, specifically the *gift of tongues*.
- We learned the Jewish day started at sunrise, or 6:00 a.m.
- We discussed the difference between a Nazarene and a Nazarite.
- We discussed the Old Testament prophecies mentioned in the first two chapters.
- We discussed salvation as it relates to baptism.

(Q) ANY OTHER COMMENTS ON THE FIRST TWO CHAPTERS?_____

STOP AND DISCUSS THE ABOVE COMMENTS.

Let's Begin Tonight's Study

> **Acts 3:1 (NASB).** [1] Now Peter and John were going up to the temple at the **ninth hour, the hour of prayer**.

Commentary. Even though Peter and John had a newfound faith in Jesus, they still continued to pray in the temple with other Jews per the Jewish custom. Also, remember it was the ninth hour of the day when Jesus cried from the cross, *"It is finished"* (John 19:30).

(Q) WHAT TIME OF DAY IS THE NINTH HOUR?_____

(Q) WHAT DO YOU KNOW ABOUT THE APOSTLES PETER AND JOHN?_____

(Q) ANY OTHER COMMENTS ON THESE VERSES?_____

STOP AND DISCUSS THE ABOVE VERSES AND QUESTIONS. Answers to questions are on the next page.

> **Acts 3:2–8 (NASB).** [2] And **a man who had been unable to walk from birth** was being carried, whom they used to set down every day at the gate of the temple which is called Beautiful, in order for him to beg for charitable gifts from those entering the temple grounds. [3] When he saw Peter and John about to go into the temple grounds, he began asking to receive a charitable gift. [4] But Peter, along with John, looked at him intently and said,
> *"Look at us!"*
> [5] And he gave them his attention, expecting to receive something from them.
> [6] But Peter said,
> *"I do not have silver and gold, but what I do have I give to you: In the name of Jesus Christ the Nazarene, walk!"*
> [7] And grasping him by the right hand, he raised him up; and **immediately his feet and his ankles were strengthened**. [8] And leaping up, he stood and began to walk; and he entered the temple with them, walking and **leaping and praising God**.

Commentary. The crippled man's ankles and feet were **physically healed** (*think about that*). The man was instantly and completely healed. It is the same way for sinners. When someone repents and puts their faith in Jesus, they are instantly saved, and their salvation is complete. The crippled man is an example of someone praying for what *they wanted* (money), only to have God give them what *they needed*.

OUR LESSON: Do I remember to thank God when a prayer has been answered? Even when it is not the way I thought or hoped it would be answered?

(Q) WHAT VERSE TELLS US THAT PETER DID NOT HEAL THE MAN?_____

(Q) ANY OTHER COMMENTS ON THESE VERSES?_____

STOP AND DISCUSS THE ABOVE VERSES AND QUESTIONS. Answers to questions are on the next page.

(Q) WHAT TIME OF DAY IS THE NINTH HOUR?

- In ancient Israel, the day started at sunrise (6:00 a.m.); therefore, the ninth hour of the day would be **3:00 p.m.**

(Q) WHAT DO YOU KNOW ABOUT THE APOSTLES PETER AND JOHN?

Jesus's closest friends were John, James, and Peter, and they were often asked to accompany Him without the other Apostles.

Peter has been described as the apostle with the *foot-shaped mouth*.

- Peter, James, and John were partners in a profitable fishing business (Luke 5:10).
- It was Peter's brother Andrew who brought Peter to follow Jesus (John 1:40–42).
- It was Peter who first declared Jesus as the Son of God (Matthew 16:16–17).
- It was Peter who was rebuked by Jesus for trying to talk Him out of going to Jerusalem to be crucified (Matthew 16:22–23).
- It was Peter who left the boat to walk on the water during a storm (Matthew 14:28–29). And it was Peter who began to sink when he took his eyes off the Lord (Matthew 14:30).
- It was Peter who was ready to take on the whole Roman army when they came to arrest Jesus (John 18:10).
- It was Peter who denied that he ever knew Jesus (Matthew 26:29–75).
- It was Peter who was intimidated by the legalists when they came to Antioch and saw him eating with Gentile Christians. Paul saw this as hypocrisy and publicly rebuked Peter (Galatians 2:11–14).
- Peter was married (1 Corinthians 9:5).
- Peter and John were given the special task of preparing the final Passover meal (Luke 22:8).
- It was Peter who suggested building three tabernacles to honor Moses, Elijah, and Jesus (Matthew 17:4).
- It was Peter, on the Day of Pentecost, who proclaimed salvation through Jesus to a crowd of three thousand, which launched the birth of the Christian church (Acts 2:41).

John was known as the Apostle of Love.

- John had a brother named James, who was also an apostle (Matthew 17:1).
- Jesus called John and James the *Sons of Thunder* because of their loud and bold personalities (Mark 3:17).
- John's father was Zebedee, and John and James are sometimes referred to as the *sons of Zebedee* (Mark 10:35).
- John referred to himself as *"the one that Jesus Loved"* (John 13:23).
- John was the only apostle not to die a martyr's death.

(Q) WHAT VERSE TELLS US THAT PETER DID NOT HEAL THE MAN?
- Verse 6b says the miracle was performed *"in the name of Jesus Christ."*

> **Acts 3:9–11 (NASB).** ⁹And all the people saw him walking and praising God; ¹⁰and they recognized him as being the very one who used to sit at the Beautiful Gate of the temple to beg for charitable gifts, and they were filled with wonder and amazement at what had happened to him. ¹¹While **he was clinging to Peter and John**, all the people ran together to them at the portico named Solomon's, completely astonished.

Commentary. The crippled man was living proof that a true miracle had occurred, and anyone who knew him could confirm the miracle. In the same way, when a sinner repents and is touched by the grace of God, he or she is a new creation, and this would be evident to all who know them. The first thing the man did was praise God and then he clung to the men that God used to heal him. We should always thank God for His blessings *and* we should remember to thank the people that helped us along the way.

(Q) How Should We Minister to a New Believer?_____

(Q) Any Other Comments on These Verses?_____

STOP AND DISCUSS THE ABOVE VERSES AND QUESTIONS. Answers to questions are on the next page.

> **Acts 3:12–16 (NASB).** ¹²But when Peter saw this, he replied to the people,
> *"Men of Israel, why are you amazed at this, or why are you staring at us, as though by our own power or godliness we had made him walk?*
> ¹³*The* **God of Abraham, Isaac, and Jacob**, *the God of our fathers, has glorified His servant Jesus, the One whom you handed over and disowned in the presence of Pilate, when he had decided to release Him.* ¹⁴*But you disowned the Holy and Righteous One, and asked for a murderer to be granted to you,* ¹⁵*but put to death the Prince of life, whom God raised from the dead, a fact to which we are witnesses.*
> ¹⁶*And on the basis of faith in His name,* **it is the name of Jesus which has strengthened this man** *whom you see and know; and the faith which comes through Him has given him this perfect health in the presence of you all."*

Commentary. Apparently, the people *thought* that Peter and John healed the crippled man. Peter used this opportunity to address the crowd and remind them that they were witnesses (v. 15b) to Jesus rising from the dead and that it was **the crippled man's faith in Jesus Christ that healed him** (v. 16b).

(Q) What Does the "*God of Abraham, Isaac, and Jacob***" Mean to the Jews?**

_____

(Q) List the Different Names Used to Describe God in These Verses?

_____

(Q) Any Other Comments on These Verses?_____

STOP AND DISCUSS THE ABOVE VERSES AND QUESTIONS. Answers to questions are on the next page.

(Q) HOW SHOULD WE MINISTER TO A NEW BELIEVER?

- Meet them where they are at, *without judgment.*
- Build the relationship.
- Pray for them.
- Encourage them.
- Show them how to study the Word of God.
- Affirm God's love for them.
- Prepare them for rough patches in their faith.

(Q) WHAT DOES the "*God of Abraham, Isaac, and Jacob*" MEAN TO THE JEWS?

- The Jews would know that the Torah says the Messiah will come through the bloodline of Abraham, Isaac, and Jacob.
- The Torah is the first five books of the Old Testament.
- God made a covenant with Abraham and his descendants, making Abraham the first Jew.
- Abraham had a son named Isaac, and Isaac had a son named Jacob, who God renamed Israel.
- The twelve tribes of Israel came from Jacob's sons and grandsons.

(Q) LIST THE DIFFERENT NAMES USED TO DESCRIBE GOD IN THESE VERSES?

- The God of Abraham, Isaac, and Jacob.
- The God of our fathers.
- Holy and Righteous One.
- Prince of life.
- Jesus.

> **Acts 3:17–21 (NASB).** ¹⁷ *"And now, brothers, I know that **you acted in ignorance, just as your rulers also did**.* ¹⁸ *But the things which God previously announced by the mouths of all the prophets, that His Christ would suffer, He has fulfilled in this way.* ¹⁹ ***Therefore repent and return, so that your sins may be wiped away, in order that times of refreshing** may come from the presence of the Lord;* ²⁰ *and that He may send Jesus, the Christ appointed for you,* ²¹ *whom heaven must receive until the period of restoration of all things, about which God spoke by the mouths of His holy prophets from ancient times."*

Commentary. Peter called the Jews ignorant, just like their leaders. He was not calling them dumb; he was saying they lacked knowledge and awareness.

(Q) In Verse 17, What Were They Ignorant Of?_____

(Q) In Verse 19b, What Does *"times of refreshing"* Mean?_____

(Q) Any Other Comments on These Verses?_____

Stop and Discuss the Above Verses and Questions. Answers to questions are on the next page.

> **Acts 3:22–26 (NASB).** ²² *"**Moses** said,*
> *'The Lord God Will Raise Up for You a Prophet Like Me*
> *from Your Countrymen;*   ← **Deuteronomy 18:15**
> *to Him You Shall Listen regarding everything he says to you.'*
> ²³ *And it shall be that every soul that does not listen to that prophet shall be utterly destroyed from among the people.* ²⁴ *And likewise, all the prophets who have spoken from **Samuel** and his successors onward, have also announced these days.* ²⁵ *It is you who are the sons of the prophets and of the covenant which God ordained with your fathers, saying to Abraham,*
> *'And in Your Seed All the Families of the Earth Shall Be Blessed.'* ← **Genesis 22:18**
> ²⁶ ***God raised up His Servant for you first**, and sent Him to bless you by turning every one of you from your wicked ways."*

Commentary. Peter continued to use the Old Testament to show that **Moses** and **Samuel** were prophesizing about the coming of Jesus and that the Messiah would come to the Jews first and then the Gentiles (v. 26).

(Q) Why Does Verse 25 Tell Us That Paul Is Talking Specifically to Jews?

_____

(Q) Who Was Samuel?_____

(Q) Any Other Comments on These Verses?_____

Stop and Discuss the Above Verses and Questions. Answers to questions are on the next page.

(Q) IN VERSE 17, WHAT WERE THEY IGNORANT OF?

- The **Jews did not recognize Jesus as the Messiah** until He rose from the dead.
- Here is how the Message Bible says it:

And now, friends, I know you had no idea what you were doing when you killed Jesus, and neither did your leaders. But God, who through the preaching of all the prophets had said all along that His Messiah would be killed, knew exactly what you were doing and used it to fulfill His plans. Now it's time to change your ways. Turn to face God so He can wipe away your sins, pour out showers of blessing to refresh you, and send you the Messiah He prepared for you, namely, Jesus. (Acts 3:17–19 MSG)

(Q) IN VERSE 19b, WHAT DOES "*times of refreshing*" MEAN?

- This refers to the **spiritual regeneration** that occurs the moment a sinner repents and gives their life to Jesus.

(Q) WHY DOES VERSE 25 TELL US THAT PAUL IS TALKING SPECIFICALLY TO JEWS?

- The verses say, "*You who are the **sons of the prophets** and of the **covenant with God**.*"
- "*You*" refers to the people listening to Peter.
- The "*sons of the prophet*" refers to the Israelites.
- The "*covenant*" refers to the covenant God made with Abraham and ultimately with the Jewish people.

(Q) WHO WAS SAMUEL?

- He was the son of Elkanah and Hannah.
- Hannah was barren and could not have children.
- Hannah made a promise to God that she would dedicate her son **if** the Lord would "open her womb."
- When Samuel was about 4 to 5 years old, Hannah kept her promise to God and took Samuel to the tabernacle to live with Eli, the priest.
- Samuel was the last judge in Israel.
- Samuel was a prophet and he anointed the first two kings of Israel.
- The main theme throughout Samuel's life is that he was obedient to God.

Let's RE-Read Tonight's Verses

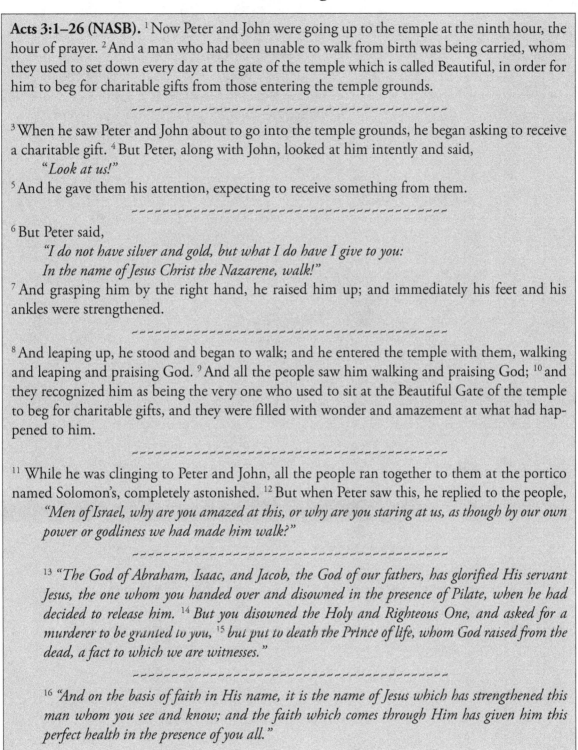

Acts 3:1–26 (NASB). [1] Now Peter and John were going up to the temple at the ninth hour, the hour of prayer. [2] And a man who had been unable to walk from birth was being carried, whom they used to set down every day at the gate of the temple which is called Beautiful, in order for him to beg for charitable gifts from those entering the temple grounds.

- -

[3] When he saw Peter and John about to go into the temple grounds, he began asking to receive a charitable gift. [4] But Peter, along with John, looked at him intently and said,
"Look at us!"
[5] And he gave them his attention, expecting to receive something from them.

- -

[6] But Peter said,
"I do not have silver and gold, but what I do have I give to you:
In the name of Jesus Christ the Nazarene, walk!"
[7] And grasping him by the right hand, he raised him up; and immediately his feet and his ankles were strengthened.

- -

[8] And leaping up, he stood and began to walk; and he entered the temple with them, walking and leaping and praising God. [9] And all the people saw him walking and praising God; [10] and they recognized him as being the very one who used to sit at the Beautiful Gate of the temple to beg for charitable gifts, and they were filled with wonder and amazement at what had happened to him.

- -

[11] While he was clinging to Peter and John, all the people ran together to them at the portico named Solomon's, completely astonished. [12] But when Peter saw this, he replied to the people,
"Men of Israel, why are you amazed at this, or why are you staring at us, as though by our own power or godliness we had made him walk?"

- -

[13] *"The God of Abraham, Isaac, and Jacob, the God of our fathers, has glorified His servant Jesus, the one whom you handed over and disowned in the presence of Pilate, when he had decided to release him. [14] But you disowned the Holy and Righteous One, and asked for a murderer to be granted to you, [15] but put to death the Prince of life, whom God raised from the dead, a fact to which we are witnesses."*

- -

[16] *"And on the basis of faith in His name, it is the name of Jesus which has strengthened this man whom you see and know; and the faith which comes through Him has given him this perfect health in the presence of you all."*

- -

> [17] "And now, brothers, I know that you acted in ignorance, just as your rulers also did. [18] But the things which God previously announced by the mouths of all the prophets, that His Christ would suffer, He has fulfilled in this way."
>
> --
>
> [19] "Therefore repent and return, so that your sins may be wiped away, in order that times of refreshing may come from the presence of the Lord; [20] and that He may send Jesus, the Christ appointed for you, [21] whom heaven must receive until the period of restoration of all things, about which God spoke by the mouths of His holy prophets from ancient times."
>
> --
>
> [22] "Moses said,
>> 'THE LORD GOD WILL RAISE UP FOR YOU A PROPHET LIKE ME FROM YOUR COUN-
>> TRYMEN; TO HIM YOU SHALL LISTEN regarding everything He says to you. [23]
>> And it shall be that every soul that does not listen to that prophet shall be
>> utterly destroyed from among the people.'
> [24] And likewise, all the prophets who have spoken from Samuel and his successors onward, have also announced these days."
>
> --
>
> [25] "It is you who are the sons of the prophets and of the covenant which God ordained with your fathers, saying to Abraham,
>> 'AND IN YOUR SEED ALL THE FAMILIES OF THE EARTH SHALL BE BLESSED.'
> [26] God raised up His Servant for you first, and sent Him to bless you by turning every one of you from your wicked ways."

(Q) ANY FINAL COMMENTS?_____

THIS IS THE END OF THIS WEEK'S STUDY.

A Precept Bible Study

ACTS

The Birth of the Church

Week 4, Acts 4:1–37

A Verse-by-Verse Journey through the book of Acts

Notes

Let's Review Last Week's Study

- God healed a crippled man *through* Peter. However, the people believed Peter healed the crippled man instead of God.
- Lessons learned from the healed man:
  - It is Jesus that heals, not man.
  - We need to give God the glory and thank Him for His blessings.
  - God's plan, is *way* better than our plans.
- Lessons learned about how to minister to a new believer:
  - Meet the new believer where they are at, without judgment.
  - Build the relationship.
  - Pray for and encourage them.
  - Show them how to study the Word of God; in other words, disciple them.
  - Affirm God's love for them and prepare them for rough patches in their faith.

(Q) ANY OTHER COMMENTS ON CHAPTER 3?_____

STOP AND DISCUSS THE ABOVE COMMENTS.

Let's Review Tonight's Study

Tonight, we will meet a group of people called the Sadducees. The Sadducees were a religio-political group that held a great deal of power among the Jews in ancient Israel. They tended to be wealthy and were rude, arrogant, and power hungry. They were quick to quarrel with those who disagreed with them.

SADDUCEES:
- Did not believe in the resurrection of the dead
- Did not believe in the afterlife
- Did not believe in a spiritual world

SANHEDRIN COUNCIL:
- A seventy-member supreme court of ancient Israel, consisting of the **Sadducees** and the **Pharisees**
- The Sadducees held the majority of seats on the Sanhedrin Council.

(Q) WHO WERE THE PHARISEES?_____

(Q) ANY OTHER COMMENTS?_____

STOP AND DISCUSS THE ABOVE COMMENTS AND QUESTION. Answer to question is on the next page.

(Q) WHO WERE THE PHARISEES?

- The Pharisees were an influential religious sect within Judaism during the time of Christ.
- They emphasized personal piety.
- They believed the oral tradition was equal to the written Law.
- They believed all Jews must observe all six hundred-plus laws in the Torah.
- They were legalistic and followed a strict, unbending interpretation of the Law.
- They believed they were pleasing God because they kept the Law.
- They believed in the resurrection of the dead.
- They believed in an afterlife.
- They believed in the spiritual world, including angels and demons.
- Some Pharisees mentioned in the Bible were Nicodemus and Gamaliel.

Let's Begin Tonight's Study

> **Acts 4:1–6 (NASB).** [1] As they were speaking to the people, the priests and the captain of the temple guard and the Sadducees came up to them, [2] being greatly disturbed because they were teaching the people and proclaiming in Jesus the resurrection from the dead. [3] And they laid hands on them and put them in prison until the next day, for it was already evening.
> [4] But **many of those who had heard the message believed; and the number of the men came to be about five thousand**. [5] On the next day, their rulers and elders and scribes were gathered together in Jerusalem; [6] and Annas the high priest was there, and Caiaphas, John, and Alexander, and all who were of high-priestly descent.

Commentary. After Peter healed the crippled man, another five thousand people came to believe and follow Jesus! The **Sadducees saw Peter and John as a threat to their authority**, so they had them arrested. Annas and Caiaphas were members of the Sanhedrin Council and were the high priests during Jesus's trial.

(Q) What Else Do We Know about Annas and Caiaphas? (Read John 18:13.)

_____

(Q) Any Other Comments on These Verses?_____

Stop and Discuss the Above Verses and Questions. Answers to question are on the next page.

> **Acts 4:7–12 (NASB).** [7] When they had placed them in the center, they began to inquire,
> *"By what power, or in what name, have you done this?"*
> [8] Then **Peter, filled with the Holy Spirit**, said to them,
> *"Rulers and elders of the people, [9] if we are on trial today for a benefit done to a sick man, as to how this man has been made well, [10] let it be known to all of you and to all the people of Israel, that by the name of Jesus Christ the Nazarene, **whom you crucified**, whom God raised from the dead—by this name this man stands here before you in good health.*
> [11] *'He is the STONE WHICH WAS REJECTED by you,*   ← *Psalm 118:22*
> *THE BUILDERS, but WHICH BECAME THE CHIEF CORNERSTONE.'*
> [12] *And there is salvation in no one else; for there is no other name under heaven that has been given among mankind by which we must be saved."*

Commentary. Peter began his defense by rephrasing the Sanhedrin's question from: *"in what name have you done this"* to *Are we on trial for healing a sick man?*

Then Peter said the crippled man was healed in the name of Jesus whom the Sanhedrin crucified and that Jesus is the chief cornerstone that was prophesied in the Old Testament. By quoting Psalm 118, the Sanhedrin would realize that Peter was accusing them of killing the Messiah.

(Q) Why Does the Bible Compare Jesus to the Cornerstone of a Building?

_____

(Q) Any Other Comments on These Verses?_____

Stop and Discuss the Above Verses and Questions. Answers to questions are on the next page.

Answers to Questions from the Previous Page

(Q) What Else Do We Know about Annas and Caiaphas?

- Annas was the high priest until he appointed his son-in-law Caiaphas to replace him.
- Since the Jews considered the high priest a lifetime position, they still referred to Annas as the high priest, and he maintained many of the rights and obligations of the high priests.
- Annas and Caiaphas played a significant role in the trial of Jesus and were probably not happy to see that Jesus's followers were just as persistent as Jesus was.
- Eventually, all five of Annas's sons would be appointed to the position of high priest.

(Q) Why Does the Bible Compare Jesus to the Cornerstone of a Building?

- The cornerstone or foundation stone is the first stone set in the construction of a masonry foundation. All other stones are set in reference to this stone; thus, the cornerstone determines the position of the entire structure.
- In the Old Testament, God promised to send His Son to be the foundation for our lives, if we trust in Him.
- Peter was telling the Sanhedrin Council that Jesus is "*the stone that you rejected*" which was prophesized in the Torah.

> **Acts 4:13–17 (NASB).** [13] Now as the [Sadducees] observed the confidence of Peter and John and understood that they were uneducated and untrained men, they were amazed, and began to recognize them as having been with Jesus. [14] And seeing the man who had been healed standing with them, they had nothing to say in reply. [15] But when they had ordered them to leave the Council, they began to confer with one another, [16] saying,
>
> *"What are we to do with these men? For **the fact that a noteworthy miracle has taken place through them is apparent to all who live in Jerusalem**, and we cannot deny it. [17] But so that it will not spread any further among the people, let's warn them not to speak any longer to any person in this name."*

Commentary. Peter and John had done nothing wrong and the Sanhedrin Council knew it. They also knew that a "*noteworthy miracle*" had occurred, and it was "*apparent to all.*" Uh-oh, time for the Sadducees to try and censor the truth, so they "*warned them not to speak this name.*" Notice that the Sadducees would not say the name of Jesus and referred to Him as "*this name.*"

(Q) WHY WERE THE SANHEDRIN AMAZED WITH PETER AND JOHN?_____

(Q) WHAT WAS THE SANHEDRIN'S SOLUTION?_____

(Q) ANY OTHER COMMENTS ON THESE VERSES?_____

STOP AND DISCUSS THE ABOVE VERSES AND QUESTIONS. **Answers to questions are on the next page.**

> **Acts 4:18–22 (NASB).** [18] And when they had summoned them, they commanded them not to speak or teach at all in the name of Jesus. [19] But Peter and John answered and said to them,
>
> *"Whether it is right in the sight of God to listen to you rather than to God, make your own judgment; [20] for **we cannot stop speaking about what we have seen and heard.**"*
>
> [21] When they had threatened them further, they let them go (finding no basis on which to punish them) on account of the people, because they were all glorifying God for what had happened; [22] for **the man on whom this miracle of healing had been performed was more than forty years old**.

Commentary. The Sanhedrin found themselves in a bind: the people in the city were glorifying Jesus because of the miracle, and **Peter and John refused to stop preaching about Jesus**. People can argue over religious doctrine, but no one can argue over a changed life.

REFLECTIVE QUESTION: Do I have a testimony that points to Jesus and the new life He gave me?

(Q) IN VERSES 22, WHY DID LUKE NEED TO MENTION THE HEALED MAN'S AGE?_____

(Q) ANY OTHER COMMENTS ON THESE VERSES?_____

STOP AND DISCUSS THE ABOVE VERSES AND QUESTIONS. **Answers to questions are on the next page.**

Answers to Questions from the Previous Page

(Q) Why Were the Sanhedrin Amazed with Peter and John?

- The members of the Sanhedrin had gone to special schools to learn the Jewish customs and the Torah. Peter and John were uneducated, common fishermen.
- The members of the Sanhedrin thought they were smarter than Peter and John and were amazed when they answered the Sanhedrin's questions *and* then explained the scriptures to them!

(Q) What Was the Sanhedrin's Solution?

- They knew they could not keep them in jail, but they did not want the apostles to tell everyone that there was power in the name of Jesus.
- So they tried to silence Peter and John by warning them not to talk about Jesus anymore.
- Of course, the apostle's response was, **"We cannot stop speaking about what we have seen and heard."**

(Q) In Verse 22, Why Did Luke Need to Mention the Healed Man's Age?

- To emphasize that this man had been crippled for his entire life.
- This would be verification that a true miracle had occurred.

Acts 4:23–31 (NASB). ²³ When they had been released, they went to their own companions and reported everything that the chief priests and the elders had said to them. ²⁴ And when they heard this, they raised their voices to God with one mind and said,

"*Lord, it is You who* MADE THE HEAVEN AND THE EARTH AND THE SEA, AND EVERYTHING THAT IS IN THEM, ²⁵ *who by the Holy Spirit, through the mouth of our father David Your servant, said,*

'WHY WERE THE NATIONS INSOLENT, ← *Psalm 2:1–2*
AND THE PEOPLES PLOTTING IN VAIN?
²⁶ THE KINGS OF THE EARTH TOOK THEIR STAND,
AND THE RULERS WERE GATHERED TOGETHER
AGAINST THE LORD AND AGAINST HIS CHRIST.'

²⁷ *For truly in this city there were gathered together against Your holy servant Jesus, whom You anointed, both* **Herod and Pontius Pilate**, *along with the Gentiles and the peoples of Israel,* ²⁸ *to do whatever Your hand and purpose predestined to occur.* ²⁹ *And now, Lord, look at their threats, and grant it to Your bond-servants to speak Your word with all confidence,* ³⁰ *while You extend Your hand to heal, and signs and wonders take place through the name of Your holy servant Jesus.*"

³¹ And when they had prayed, the place where they had gathered together was shaken, and they were all filled with the Holy Spirit and began to speak the word of God with boldness.

Commentary. After Peter and John were released, they went to their companions and prayed with them. Their prayer began by acknowledging God as the Creator of all things. Then they quoted Psalm 2, which was a prophecy about kings and rulers plotting against the Messiah. This prophecy was fulfilled when Herod and Pontius Pilate sentenced Jesus to die on a cross. There are many Herods in the Bible; this Herod was Herod Antipas.

(Q) IN VERSE 27, WHO WAS HEROD ANTIPAS?_____

(Q) WHAT DID PETER AND JOHN ASK FOR IN THEIR PRAYER?_____

(Q) ANY OTHER COMMENTS ON THESE VERSES?_____

STOP AND DISCUSS THE ABOVE VERSES AND QUESTIONS. **Answers to questions are on the next page.**

(Q) IN VERSE 27, WHO WAS HEROD ANTIPAS?

The name Herod was a title that meant "ruler." So it is easy to get confused with all the Herods mentioned in the Bible. Let's try to clarify who's who:

- **Herod Antipas** was king when John the Baptist was beheaded. Later, he declined to pass judgement on Jesus and sent Him back to Pilate (Acts 4). He was known as **Herod the tetrarch** (Acts 13). He eventually fell out of favor with Rome and was exiled to Gaul.

Here are some other Herods mentioned in the Bible.

- **Herod the Great.** He was king when Jesus was born, and ordered the slaughter of the firstborn boys in Bethlehem in an effort to kill the Messiah.
- **Herod Agrippa I.** He was the grandson of Herod the Great and the nephew of Herod Antipas. He had James, the brother of John, beheaded and then threw Peter in jail with the intention of killing him. When an angel of the Lord freed Peter from jail, Herod was so angry, he left Judea and went to Caesarea. While he was in Caesarea giving a speech, the people began yelling, "*He has the voice of a god and not of a man.*" When Agrippa did not "*give God the glory,*" an "*angel of the Lord struck him down*" and then "*he was eaten by worms and died*" *(Acts 12)*.
- **Herod Agrippa II.** He was the son of King Herod Agrippa I and was married to Bernice. Bernice was Agrippa II's sister, who was also previously married to her uncle, Herod Antipas. She was also the sister of Drusilla, who was married to Governor Felix, making Felix and Festus brothers-in-law. King Agrippa II and his wife Bernice were both Jews (Acts 27).

(Q) WHAT DID PETER AND JOHN ASK FOR IN THEIR PRAYER?

Lord, look at their threats, and grant it to Your bond-servants to speak Your word with all confidence, while You extend Your hand to heal, and signs and wonders take place through the name of Your holy servant Jesus (Acts 4:29–30).

- They asked for confidence so they could boldly speak the word of God.
- They asked God to use them to heal people.
- They asked God to use them to perform signs and wonders.

> **Acts 4:32–37 (NASB).** [32] And the congregation of those who believed were of one heart and soul; and not one of them claimed that anything belonging to him was his own, but **all things were common property** to them.
>
> [33] And with great power the apostles were giving testimony to the resurrection of the Lord Jesus, and abundant grace was upon them all. [34] For there was not a needy person among them, for all who were owners of land or houses would sell them and bring the proceeds of the sales [35] and lay them at the apostles' feet, and **they would be distributed to each to the extent that any had need**.
>
> [36] Now Joseph, a Levite of Cyprian birth, who was also called Barnabas by the apostles (which translated means Son of Encouragement), [37] owned a tract of land. So, he sold it, and brought the money and laid it at the apostles' feet.

Commentary. The early church shared their possessions, eliminating poverty among them (v. 34). Their attitude was that everything comes from God, and they were only sharing what was already God's. Their generosity and unity were brought on by the power of the Holy Spirit, working in and through the believer's lives. The early Christians brought their money and possessions to the apostles, and then the apostles redistributed the goods among the church members, based on need. This sounds like socialism, right?

This is the first mention of Barnabas, who also contributed money after selling some land. Later on, we'll read about Barnabas and the Apostle Paul's adventures in Galatia as they preached the good news.

(Q) WHAT IS THE DIFFERENCE BETWEEN "CHRISTIAN SOCIALISM" AND "POLITICAL SOCIALISM"?

_____

(Q) WHO WAS BARNABAS?_____

(Q) ANY OTHER COMMENTS ON THESE VERSES?_____

STOP AND DISCUSS THE ABOVE VERSES AND QUESTIONS. **Answers to questions are on the next page.**

(Q) What Is the Difference between "Christian Socialism" and "Political Socialism"?

Political socialism:

- An economic and political system in which property, natural resources and the means of production are owned and managed by the government rather than by individuals or private companies.
- In this system, wealth is **involuntarily** taken from the rich and redistributed to the poor so that the wealth is spread out equally.

Christian socialism in the early church:

- In this system, people **voluntarily** share their money and possessions with the less fortunate.
- The church manages and distributes goods, not the government.
- There are no Bible verses that call for a mandate to redistribute wealth; however, God does command Christians to give to the less fortunate.

  Each one must do just as he has decided in his heart, not reluctantly or under compulsion, for God loves a cheerful giver. (2 Corinthians 9:7)

  From everyone who has been given much, much will be demanded; and to whom they entrusted much, of him they will ask all the more. (Luke 12:48)

(Q) Who Was Barnabas?

- He was a *"good man, full of the Holy Spirit and faith"* (Acts 11:24).
- He was an encourager (Acts 4:36).
- Barnabas brought Paul to the apostles when they did not believe he was a follower of Christ (Acts 9:27).
- He accompanied Paul on his first missionary trip (Acts 13).
- Barnabas and the Apostle Paul started the first Gentile church in Antioch (Acts 11:25–30).
- John Mark and Barnabas were cousins (John Mark wrote the Gospel of Mark).
- Barnabas mentored John Mark and took him on a missionary journey.

Let's RE-Read Tonight's Verses

Acts 4:1–37 (NASB). [1] As they were speaking to the people, the priests and the captain of the temple guard and the Sadducees came up to them, [2] being greatly disturbed because they were teaching the people and proclaiming in Jesus the resurrection from the dead.

[3] And they laid hands on them and put them in prison until the next day, for it was already evening. [4] But many of those who had heard the message believed; and the number of the men came to be about five thousand.

[5] On the next day, their rulers and elders and scribes were gathered together in Jerusalem; [6] and Annas the high priest was there, and Caiaphas, John, and Alexander, and all who were of high-priestly descent.
[7] When they had placed them in the center, they began to inquire,
"By what power, or in what name, have you done this?"

[8] Then Peter, filled with the Holy Spirit, said to them,
"Rulers and elders of the people, [9] *if we are on trial today for a benefit done to a sick man, as to how this man has been made well,* [10] *let it be known to all of you and to all the people of Israel, that by the name of Jesus Christ the Nazarene, whom you crucified, whom God raised from the dead—by this name this man stands here before you in good health.*
[11] *'He is the* STONE WHICH WAS REJECTED *by you,* THE BUILDERS,
but WHICH BECAME THE CHIEF CORNERSTONE.*'*
[12] *And there is salvation in no one else; for there is no other name under heaven that has been given among mankind by which we must be saved."*

[13] Now as they observed the confidence of Peter and John and understood that they were uneducated and untrained men, they were amazed, and began to recognize them as having been with Jesus. [14] And seeing the man who had been healed standing with them, they had nothing to say in reply.

[15] But when they had ordered them to leave the Council, they began to confer with one another, [16] saying,
"What are we to do with these men? For the fact that a noteworthy miracle has taken place through them is apparent to all who live in Jerusalem, and we cannot deny it. [17] *But so that it will not spread any further among the people, let's warn them not to speak any longer to any person in this name."*

[18] And when they had summoned them, they commanded them not to speak or teach at all in the name of Jesus. [19] But Peter and John answered and said to them,

"Whether it is right in the sight of God to listen to you rather than to God, make your own judgment; [20] for we cannot stop speaking about what we have seen and heard."

- -

[21] When they had threatened them further, they let them go (finding no basis on which to punish them) on account of the people, because they were all glorifying God for what had happened; [22] for the man on whom this miracle of healing had been performed was more than forty years old.

- -

[23] When they had been released, they went to their own companions and reported everything that the chief priests and the elders had said to them. [24] And when they heard this, they raised their voices to God with one mind and said,

"Lord, it is You who MADE THE HEAVEN AND THE EARTH AND THE SEA, AND EVERYTHING THAT IS IN THEM*"*

- -

[25] *"Who by the Holy Spirit, through the mouth of our father David Your servant, said,*

'WHY WERE THE NATIONS INSOLENT,
AND THE PEOPLES PLOTTING IN VAIN?
[26] THE KINGS OF THE EARTH TOOK THEIR STAND,
AND THE RULERS WERE GATHERED TOGETHER
AGAINST THE LORD AND AGAINST HIS CHRIST.'"

- -

[27] *"For truly in this city there were gathered together against Your holy servant Jesus, whom You anointed, both Herod and Pontius Pilate, along with the Gentiles and the peoples of Israel, [28] to do whatever Your hand and purpose predestined to occur. [29] And now, Lord, look at their threats, and grant it to Your bond-servants to speak Your word with all confidence, [30] while You extend Your hand to heal, and signs and wonders take place through the name of Your holy servant Jesus."*

- -

[31] And when they had prayed, the place where they had gathered together was shaken, and they were all filled with the Holy Spirit and began to speak the word of God with boldness. [32] And the congregation of those who believed were of one heart and soul; and not one of them claimed that anything belonging to him was his own, but all things were common property to them.

- -

[33] And with great power the apostles were giving testimony to the resurrection of the Lord Jesus, and abundant grace was upon them all. [34] For there was not a needy person among them, for all who were owners of land or houses would sell them and bring the proceeds of the sales [35] and lay them at the apostles' feet, and they would be distributed to each to the extent that any had need.

- -

> [36] Now Joseph, a Levite of Cyprian birth, who was also called Barnabas by the apostles (which translated means Son of Encouragement), [37] owned a tract of land. So he sold it, and brought the money and laid it at the apostles' feet.

(Q) ANY FINAL COMMENTS?_____

THIS IS THE END OF THIS WEEK'S STUDY.

A Precept Bible Study

ACTS

The Birth of the Church

Week 5, Acts 5:1–42

A Verse-by-Verse Journey through the book of Acts

Let's Review Last Week's Study

- Peter gave a sermon and five thousand men came to believe in Jesus Christ (many more if you count their wives and families).
- After God used Peter to heal a crippled man, word spread throughout the city and the Sadducees saw this as a threat to their authority and had Peter and John arrested. Then they brought them to trial before the Sanhedrin Council.
- During his defense, Peter quoted the Old Testament to show that Jesus was prophesized as *"the Chief Cornerstone that the Builders rejected."*
- The Sanhedrin Council got angry and warned Peter and John to quit talking about Jesus. Peter and John's response was, *"We cannot stop speaking about what we have seen and heard."*
- Last week ended with the believers giving their wealth and possessions to the apostles so they could redistribute the goods among the church members, based on need. Some people have referred to this as a form of *Christian socialism.*
- We met Barnabas for the first time when he sold his land and gave **all** the profits to the apostles.

(Q) Any Other Comments on Chapter 4?_____

Stop and Discuss the Above Comments.

Let's Review Tonight's Study

Before we read tonight's verses, let's meet some of the people that will be mentioned in this chapter:

Ananias and Sapphira
- They were a wealthy married couple and members of the church.

Gamaliel
- He was a Jewish Rabbi and a leader in the Sanhedrin Council.
- He was a Pharisee and a grandson of the famous Rabbi Hillel.
- He was Saul of Tarsus's rabbi (teacher).

Theudas
- He was a false prophet and was known by the Romans as a troublemaker.
- Gamaliel used Theudas as an example of a false messiah, who once had many followers but soon faded away when his followers killed him.

(Q) Any Other Comments on These People?_____

Stop and Discuss the Above Comments.

Let's Begin Tonight's Study

> **Acts 5:1–11 (NASB).** [1] But **a man named Ananias, with his wife Sapphira, sold a piece of property,** [2] **and kept back some of the proceeds for himself, with his wife's full knowledge,** and bringing a portion of it, he laid it at the apostles' feet. [3] But Peter said,
>
> *"Ananias, why has Satan filled your heart to lie to the Holy Spirit and to keep back some of the proceeds of the land? [4] While it remained unsold, did it not remain your own? And after it was sold, was it not under your control? Why is it that you have conceived this deed in your heart? You have not lied to men, but to God."*
>
> [5] And as he heard these words, Ananias collapsed and died; and great fear came over all who heard about it. [6] The young men got up and covered him up, and after carrying him out, they buried him. [7] Now an interval of about three hours elapsed, and his wife came in, not knowing what had happened. [8] And Peter responded to her, *"Tell me whether you sold the land for this price?"* And she said, *"Yes, for that price."*
>
> [9] Then Peter said to her,
>
> *"Why is it that you have agreed together to put the Spirit of the Lord to the test? Behold, the feet of those who have buried your husband are at the door, and they will carry you out as well."*
>
> [10] And immediately she collapsed at his feet and died; and the young men came in and found her dead, and they carried her out and buried her beside her husband. [11] And great fear came over the whole church, and over all who heard about these things.

Commentary. So far, we have been reading about the birth of the Christian church during a time of great persecution and growth. As the church grew, so did the problems. This chapter begins with Peter addressing a problem with a couple of members.

(Q) WHY WERE ANANIAS AND SAPPHIRA JUDGED SO HARSHLY?_____

(Q) ANY OTHER COMMENTS ON THESE VERSES?_____

REFLECTIVE QUESTION: Do I use social media to make myself look more spiritual or exaggerate my accomplishments to appear more successful just to impress others?

STOP AND DISCUSS THE ABOVE VERSES AND QUESTIONS. Answers to questions are on the next page.

> **Acts 5:12–13 (NASB).** [12] At the hands of the apostles many signs and wonders were taking place among the people; and they were all together in Solomon's portico. [13] **But none of the rest dared to associate with them;** however, the people held them in high esteem.

Commentary. The people held the apostles in high esteem. However, the crowds kept their distance from the apostles and did *not dare to associate with them.*

(Q) WHY WOULD THE PEOPLE BE AFRAID TO *associate with the apostles?* _____

(Q) ANY OTHER COMMENTS ON THESE VERSES?_____

STOP AND DISCUSS THE ABOVE VERSES AND QUESTIONS. Answers to questions are on the next page.

Answers to Questions from the Previous Page

(Q) Why Were Ananias and Sapphira Judged so Harshly?

- The sin Ananias and Sapphira committed was not stinginess or even holding back part of the money. Peter acknowledged that it was their choice to sell their land and how much they should give.
- Their sin was **lying** to God and to God's people to make themselves appear more generous than they really were. In that sense, the root of their sin was **pride**.
- This act was judged harshly because dishonesty prevents the Holy Spirit from working effectively and destroys our relationship with God.

(Q) Why Would the People Be Afraid to *associate with the apostles?*

- Some were afraid to face the same persecution as the apostles.
- Some were afraid to face the same fate as Ananias and Sapphira.
- God's judgment on Ananias and Sapphira made the people realize how serious God regarded sin.

> **Acts 5:14–16 (NASB).** ¹⁴And increasingly believers in the Lord, large numbers of men and women, were being added to their number, ¹⁵to such an extent that they even carried the sick out into the streets and laid them on cots and pallets, so that when Peter came by at least his shadow might fall on any of them. ¹⁶The people from the cities in the vicinity of Jerusalem were coming together as well, bringing people who were sick or tormented with unclean spirits, and they were all being healed.

Commentary. You may think, How crazy for people to believe Peter's shadow could heal them, and that this could not possibly happen today, *right*? *Think again…* there are televangelist that promise to send you a "special cloth" or bottle of "holy water" that can heal you for only $29.95. Unfortunately, some Christians believe that an object can heal them, rather than faith in Jesus Christ.

(Q) What Does Verse 16b Mean, *"tormented with unclean spirits"?*_____

(Q) Is There a Difference between the *woman who was healed by touching Jesus's garment* **and the People Who** *believed Peter's shadow could heal them?* (Read Mark 5:25–34, Luke 8:43–48.)

_____

(Q) Any Other Comments on These Verses?_____

Stop and Discuss the Above Verses and Questions. Answers to questions are on the next page.

> **Acts 5:17–21 (NASB).** ¹⁷But the high priest stood up, along with all his associates (that is the sect of the **Sadducees**), and **they were filled with jealousy.** ¹⁸They laid hands on the apostles and put them in a public prison. ¹⁹But during the night an **angel of the Lord opened the gates of the prison**, and leading them out, he said,
> ²⁰*"Go, stand and speak to the people in the temple area the whole message of this Life."*
> ²¹Upon hearing this, they entered into the temple area about daybreak and began to teach.

Commentary. Jealousy is a terrible thing. The Sadducees were envies of the large crowds and adoration they saw the apostles were getting. In the previous chapter, the Sadducees had Peter and John arrested. This time, they had ALL of the apostles arrested. After the angel freed them, imagine how much courage it must have taken for the apostles to go back to the same place where they were arrested and start preaching again!

(Q) What Does Verse 20 Mean, *"speak to the people…the whole message of this life"?*

_____

(Q) How Is It Possible That These Same Apostles Who Ran Away When Jesus Was Hung from a Cross Are Now Boldly Preaching about Jesus in the Face of Persecution?

_____

(Q) Any Other Comments on These Verses?_____

Stop and Discuss the Above Verses and Questions. Answers to questions are on the next page.

(Q) WHAT DOES VERSE 16b MEAN, *"tormented with unclean spirits"?*

- It means they were possessed and tormented by **evil spirits**.

(Q) IS THERE A DIFFERENCE BETWEEN THE *woman who was healed by touching Jesus's garment* AND THE PEOPLE WHO *believed Peter's shadow could heal them?*

- The Gospel of Mark and the Gospel of Luke say the same thing about Jesus's response to the woman after being healed by touching His garment:
  ○ Jesus said to her, *"Daughter, **your faith has made you well**; go in peace and be cured of your disease"* (Mark 5:34).
  ○ Jesus said to her, "Daughter, **your faith has made you well**; go in peace" (Luke 8:48).
- Therefore, it is **faith in Jesus that heals,** *not* a garment or a shadow.

(Q) WHAT DOES VERSE 20 MEAN, *"speak to the people…the whole message of this life"?*

- The *"message of life"* refers to the life that only Jesus can give. Anyone can have this new life, if they put their faith in Jesus Christ.
- The Gospels are sometimes referred to as the *word of life*. Therefore, this verse could be saying, "tell people about Jesus."

(Q) HOW IS IT POSSIBLE THAT THESE SAME APOSTLES WHO RAN AWAY WHEN JESUS WAS HUNG FROM A CROSS ARE NOW BOLDLY PREACHING ABOUT JESUS IN THE FACE OF PERSECUTION?

- By the power of the Holy Spirit
- They had firsthand knowledge that Jesus rose from the dead and was the Messiah prophesized in the Old Testament.

> **Acts 5:21b–28 (NASB).** Now when the high priest and his associates came, they called the Council together, that is, all the Senate of the sons of Israel, and sent orders to the prison for them to be brought. ²² But the officers who came did not find them in the prison; and they returned and reported, ²³ saying,
> > *"We found the prison locked quite securely and the guards standing at the doors; but when we opened them, we found no one inside."*
> ²⁴ Now when the captain of the temple guard and the chief priests heard these words, they were greatly perplexed about them as to what would come of this. ²⁵ But someone came and reported to them,
> > ***"The men whom you put in prison are standing in the temple area and teaching the people!"***
> ²⁶ Then the captain went along with the officers and proceeded to bring them back without violence (for they were afraid of the people, that they might be stoned). ²⁷ When they had brought them, they had them stand before the Council. The high priest interrogated them, ²⁸ saying,
> > *"We gave you strict orders not to continue teaching in this name, and yet, you have filled Jerusalem with your teaching and intend to bring **this Man**'s blood upon us."*

Commentary. There is something funny about Peter and John escaping from prison, and instead of hiding, they went back to the temple area and began preaching in plain view. No wonder the officers and Jewish leaders were confused. In verse 28b, the high priest refused to say the name Jesus and referred to Jesus as *"this Man."* It is still like that today. Just mentioning the name of Jesus will send some people into rage because they are spiritually dead.

(Q) Why Would the Sanhedrin Council Be Afraid of the People, If They Were the Supreme Court for the Jews?_____

(Q) Any Other Comments on These Verses?_____

Stop and Discuss the Above Verses and Questions. Answers to questions are on the next page.

> **Acts 5:29–32 (NASB).** ²⁹ But Peter and the apostles answered,
> > ***"We must obey God rather than men***. ³⁰ *The God of our fathers raised up Jesus, whom you put to death by hanging Him on a cross.* ³¹ *He is the one whom God exalted to His right hand as a Prince and a Savior, to grant repentance to Israel, and forgiveness of sins.* ³² *And we are witnesses of these things; and so is the Holy Spirit, whom God has given to those who obey Him."*

Commentary. In these verses, Peter flat out refused to quit talking about Jesus and told the council, *"We must obey God rather than men."* In other words, he was telling the council they were not the highest authority. Then Peter outlined the Gospel message that he and the apostles were preaching.

(Q) What Is the Gospel Message Outlined in These Verses?_____

(Q) Any Other Comments on These Verses?_____

Stop and Discuss the Above Verses and Questions. Answers to questions are on the next page.

Answers to Questions from the Previous Page

(Q) Why Would the Sanhedrin Council Be Afraid of the People If They Were the supreme court for the Jews?

- The Jews had an agreement with Rome that Rome would stay out of their business as long as the Sanhedrin controlled the people.
- They were afraid of losing control of the people and losing their position of power.

(Q) What Is the Gospel Message Outlined in These Verses?

1. God sent His Son, Jesus, whom the Israelites killed (Acts 5:30).
2. God raised Him from the dead (Acts 5:30).
3. God placed Him in a high position as Ruler and Savior (Acts 5:31).
4. If people repent, God will forgive them and they will receive the Holy Spirit (Acts 5:31).
5. The apostles knew this because they had firsthand knowledge (Acts 5:32).

> **Acts 5:33–39 (NASB).** ³³ But when they heard this, they became infuriated and nearly decided to execute them. ³⁴ But **a Pharisee named Gamaliel, a teacher of the Law, respected by all the people**, stood up in the Council and gave orders to put the men outside for a short time. ³⁵ And he said to them,
>
> *"Men of Israel, be careful as to what you are about to do with these men. ³⁶ For, some time ago Theudas appeared, claiming to be somebody, and a group of about four hundred men joined him. But he was killed, and all who followed him were dispersed and came to nothing. ³⁷ After this man, Judas of Galilee appeared in the days of the census and drew away some people after him; he also perished, and all those who followed him were scattered.*
>
> ³⁸ *And so in the present case,* **I say to you, stay away from these men and leave them alone,** *for if the source of this plan or movement is men, it will be overthrown;* ³⁹ *but if the source is God, you will not be able to overthrow them; or else you may even be found fighting against God."*

Commentary. Gamaliel was an important leader in the Sanhedrin Council. He was also the Apostle Paul's teacher when Paul was known as Saul of Tarsus. Gamaliel's argument to let the apostles go was that if God was the source of their success, then they will "*not be able to overthrow them.*"

But is this true? Can people be successful without God? It depends on your definition of success. For example, there are many religions that worship false gods that have large followings.

(Q) WHY ARE THERE SO MANY RELIGIONS AND CHURCHES SUCCESSFUL WITHOUT JESUS?

_____

(Q) ANY OTHER COMMENTS ON THESE VERSES?_____

STOP AND DISCUSS THE ABOVE VERSES AND QUESTIONS. Answers to questions are on the next page.

> **Acts 5:40–42 (NASB).** ⁴⁰ They followed [Gamaliel's] advice; and after calling the apostles in, they flogged them and ordered them not to speak in the name of Jesus, and then released them. ⁴¹ So they went on their way from the presence of the Council, **rejoicing** that they had been considered worthy to suffer shame for His name. ⁴² And every day, in the temple and from house to house, **they did not stop teaching and preaching the good news of Jesus as the Christ**.

Commentary. As punishment, the apostles were *probably* flogged thirty-nine times, and yet they still rejoiced and continued preaching the name of Jesus. The apostles considered it a privilege to suffer in the name of Jesus, and they exhibited great faith and courage to preach in the temple again after being arrested and beaten multiple times.

Our Lesson: "*Charge every Christian to speak boldly in Christ's name, according as he has opportunity, and especially to take care of this tendency of our flesh to be afraid*" (Charles Spurgeon).

(Q) WHAT IS THE SIGNIFICANCE OF BEING WHIPPED THIRTY-NINE TIMES?_____

(Q) ANY OTHER COMMENTS ON THESE VERSES?_____

STOP AND DISCUSS THE ABOVE VERSES AND QUESTIONS. Answers to questions are on the next page.

(Q) Why are there so many religions and churches successful without Jesus?

- Before answering this question, we need to define success.
  - A biblical definition of success would be spending eternity in heaven with Jesus and, while on earth, obeying Jesus's commands to love God, love others, and share the good news.
  - A secular or worldly definition of success might be any number of things such as acquiring material wealth or climbing the corporate ladder. Some churches might count church growth as a measure of success regardless of how growth is achieved.
- The Apostle Paul warned Timothy about this when he wrote, *"For the time will come when they will not tolerate sound doctrine; but wanting to have their ears tickled, they will accumulate for themselves teachers in accordance with their own desires"* (2 Timothy 4:3).
- In other words, some people will follow spiritual leaders who redefine God and sin into something that supports their sinful behavior. In addition, some pastors will avoid preaching about sin or the need for repentance while focusing on church growth and programs instead. They will preach a feel-good, watered-down message that is directed at growth rather than discipling believers on the Word of God.
- Two of the more popular movements are based on universalism and relative moralism.
  - **Universalism** is the belief that all religions will lead to the same god, and everyone will go to heaven. Therefore, it doesn't matter which god you worship.
  - **Relative moralism** is the belief that morality changes with the culture and is not absolute. Therefore, the Bible is just an old book that is no longer relevant with the times.
- Obviously, NOT all religions lead to the same god, and NOT everyone will go to heaven. And God's Word is absolute and does not change with the culture as relative moralist believe.
- The Bible predicted this would happen. What we, as Christians, need to do is stay true to God's Word and keep sharing our testimony that points to Jesus Christ and our need for a savior.
- Worldly success does not guarantee a place in heaven. The only ticket to heaven is through Jesus Christ.

(Q) What Is the Significance of Being Whipped thirty-nine Times?

- It was believed if someone was whipped/flogged more than forty times, the person would die. So the Romans would whip a prisoner thirty-nine times for maximum pain without killing them.

Forty stripes he may give him, and not exceed: lest, if he should exceed, and beat him above these with many stripes, then thy brother should seem vile unto thee. (Deuteronomy 25:3 KJV)

[Paul said] Five times I received from the Jews the forty lashes minus one. (1 Corinthians 11:23 NIV)

Let's RE-Read Tonight's Verses

Acts 5:1–42 (NASB). [1] But a man named Ananias, with his wife Sapphira, sold a piece of property, [2] and kept back some of the proceeds for himself, with his wife's full knowledge, and bringing a portion of it, he laid it at the apostles' feet.

~~~~~~

[3] But Peter said,

"Ananias, why has Satan filled your heart to lie to the Holy Spirit and to keep back some of the proceeds of the land? [4] *While it remained unsold, did it not remain your own? And after it was sold, was it not under your control? Why is it that you have conceived this deed in your heart? You have not lied to men, but to God."*

~~~~~~

[5] And as he heard these words, Ananias collapsed and died; and great fear came over all who heard about it. [6] The young men got up and covered him up, and after carrying him out, they buried him. [7] Now an interval of about three hours elapsed, and his wife came in, not knowing what had happened.

~~~~~~

[8] And Peter responded to her,

"Tell me whether you sold the land for this price?"
And she said,
"Yes, for that price."
[9] Then Peter said to her,

"Why is it that you have agreed together to put the Spirit of the Lord to the test? Behold, the feet of those who have buried your husband are at the door, and they will carry you out as well."

~~~~~~

[10] And immediately she collapsed at his feet and died; and the young men came in and found her dead, and they carried her out and buried her beside her husband. [11] And great fear came over the whole church, and over all who heard about these things.

~~~~~~

[12] At the hands of the apostles many signs and wonders were taking place among the people; and they were all together in Solomon's portico. [13] But none of the rest dared to associate with them; however, the people held them in high esteem.

~~~~~~

[14] And increasingly believers in the Lord, large numbers of men and women, were being added to their number, [15] to such an extent that they even carried the sick out into the streets and laid them on cots and pallets, so that when Peter came by at least his shadow might fall on any of them.

~~~~~~

^{18} They laid hands on the apostles and put them in a public prison. ^{19} But during the night an angel of the Lord opened the gates of the prison, and leading them out, he said,

^{20} *"Go, stand and speak to the people in the temple area the whole message of this Life."*

^{21} Upon hearing this, they entered into the temple area about daybreak and began to teach.

- -

Now when the high priest and his associates came, they called the Council together, that is, all the Senate of the sons of Israel, and sent orders to the prison for them to be brought. ^{22} But the officers who came did not find them in the prison; and they returned and reported, ^{23} saying,

"We found the prison locked quite securely and the guards standing at the doors; but when we opened them, we found no one inside."

- -

^{24} Now when the captain of the temple guard and the chief priests heard these words, they were greatly perplexed about them as to what would come of this. ^{25} But someone came and reported to them,

"The men whom you put in prison are standing in the temple area and teaching the people!"

- -

^{26} Then the captain went along with the officers and proceeded to bring them back without violence (for they were afraid of the people, that they might be stoned). ^{27} When they had brought them, they had them stand before the Council.

- -

The high priest interrogated them, ^{28} saying,

"We gave you strict orders not to continue teaching in this name, and yet, you have filled Jerusalem with your teaching and intend to bring this Man's blood upon us."

- -

^{29} But Peter and the apostles answered,

"We must obey God rather than men. ^{30} The God of our fathers raised up Jesus, whom you put to death by hanging Him on a cross. ^{31} He is the one whom God exalted to His right hand as a Prince and a Savior, to grant repentance to Israel, and forgiveness of sins. ^{32} And we are witnesses of these things; and so is the Holy Spirit, whom God has given to those who obey Him."

- -

^{33} But when they heard this, they became infuriated and nearly decided to execute them. ^{34} But a Pharisee named Gamaliel, a teacher of the Law, respected by all the people, stood up in the Council and gave orders to put the men outside for a short time.

- -

^{35} And he said to them,

"Men of Israel, be careful as to what you are about to do with these men. ^{36} For, some time ago Theudas appeared, claiming to be somebody, and a group of about four hundred men joined him. But he was killed, and all who followed him were dispersed and came to nothing."

- -

> [37] *"After this man, Judas of Galilee appeared in the days of the census and drew away some people after him; he also perished, and all those who followed him were scattered.* [38] *And so in the present case, I say to you, stay away from these men and leave them alone, for if the source of this plan or movement is men, it will be overthrown;* [39] *but if the source is God, you will not be able to overthrow them; or else you may even be found fighting against God."*
>
> ~~~~~~
>
> [40] They followed his advice; and after calling the apostles in, they flogged them and ordered them not to speak in the name of Jesus, and then released them. [41] So they went on their way from the presence of the Council, rejoicing that they had been considered worthy to suffer shame for His name. [42] And every day, in the temple and from house to house, they did not stop teaching and preaching the good news of Jesus as the Christ.

(Q) ANY FINAL COMMENTS?_____

THIS IS THE END OF THIS WEEK'S STUDY.

A Precept Bible Study

ACTS

The Birth of the Church

Week 6, Acts 6:1–15, 7:1–8

A Verse-by-Verse Journey through the book of Acts

Let's Review the First Five Chapters

The book of Acts began with the events that happened *after* the death and resurrection of Jesus and describes the birth of the Christian church. **Here are some key points from the first five chapters:**

- Chapter 1 began during Passover, when Jesus appeared for forty days after His resurrection.
- Jesus told the apostles to wait in Jerusalem for the Holy Spirit to come.
- While the apostles were waiting, they appointed Matthias to replace Judas as the twelfth apostle.
- Chapter 2 described the events that occurred during Pentecost, when the Holy Spirit came upon the apostles and gave them power to speak/preach in foreign languages.
- After the Holy Spirit came, Peter gave a sermon that proved Jesus was the Messiah who was prophesized in the Torah. When Peter finished his sermon, *three thousand men* decided to follow Jesus. **This is commonly referred to as the Birth of the Church.**
- During Peter's next sermon, another five thousand men decided to follow Jesus.
- The Sadducees became jealous and were threatened by the large crowds following Peter and John, so they had them falsely arrested.
- Since the Sadducees did not have any evidence, they had to release them.
- After Peter and John were released from jail, they healed a crippled man.
- Once again, the Sadducees had Peter and John arrested, as well as all of the apostles.
- During the night, an angel of God released all the apostles from jail. After the apostles were freed, they boldly returned to the temple to preach about Jesus.
- For the third time, the Sadducees had the apostles arrested, this time they flogged them.
- A Pharisee named Gamaliel convinced the Sadducees to release the apostles and to leave them alone.
- The early Christians began giving their money and possessions to the apostles so that the apostles could redistribute the goods, based on need.
- As the church grew so did the problems. The first problem occurred when a rich couple named Ananias and Sapphira sold some property, then lied about how much they gave to the church to make themselves look more charitable. God struck them down for their *dishonesty*.

(Q) ANY OTHER COMMENTS?_____

STOP AND DISCUSS THE ABOVE COMMENTS.

Let's Review Tonight's Study

In tonight's chapter, we'll read about two more problems facing the early church:

1. Some Jewish believers were upset with the unfair distribution of goods to the Jewish widows who lived outside of Judea.
2. Jealousy arose after the apostles selected seven men to oversee the distribution of goods. By assigning ministers and deacons to handle the nonpreaching activities, the apostles were building a management structure that is still used by many churches today.

(Q) DESCRIBE HOW MOSES USED THIS SAME MANAGEMENT STRUCTURE IN THE WILDERNESS.

_____

(Q) ANY OTHER COMMENTS?_____

STOP AND DISCUSS THE ABOVE COMMENTS AND QUESTIONS. **Answer to questions are on the next page.**

Answers to Questions from the Previous Page

(Q) Describe How Moses Used This Same Management Structure In The Wilderness.

- After the Israelites were freed from slavery, Moses was responsible for overseeing the spiritual and physical needs of the people.
- This was too much work for one person, so Moses distributed the workload when his father in-law, Jethro, suggested he assign men to help him take care of the Israelites in the desert.

Moses chose able men out of all Israel and made them heads over the people, leaders of thousands, of hundreds, of fifties, and of tens. Then they judged the people at all times; they would bring the difficult matter to Moses, but they would judge every minor matter themselves. (Exodus 18:25–26)

Let's Begin Tonight's Study

> **Acts 6:1 (NASB).** [1] Now at this time, as the disciples were increasing in number, **a complaint developed on the part of the Hellenistic Jews against the native Hebrews**, because their widows were being overlooked in the daily serving of food.

Commentary. As the church grew, problems began occurring. The next problem had to do with the Jewish custom of taking care of women who had lost their husbands and had no regular income. The problem was the apostles were being accused of not taking care of the Hellenistic Jewish widows as well as they were taking care of the native Hebrew widows.

(Q) WHO WERE THE *native Hebrew widows?*_____

(Q) WHO WERE THE *Hellenistic Jewish widows?*_____

(Q) ANY OTHER COMMENTS ON THESE VERSES?_____

STOP AND DISCUSS THE ABOVE VERSES AND QUESTIONS. **Answers to questions are on the next page.**

> **Acts 6:2–4 (NASB).** [2] So the twelve [apostles] summoned the congregation of the disciples and said,
> *"It is not desirable for us to neglect the word of God in order to serve tables. [3] Instead, brothers and sisters, **select from among you seven men** of good reputation, full of the Spirit and of wisdom, whom we may put in charge of this task. [4] But we will devote ourselves to prayer and to the ministry of the word."*

Commentary. The apostles listed the requirements for selecting seven men to serve the people. These seven men would become the **first ministers/deacons in the church**. The three requirements were: (1) they must have a good reputation, (2) be full of the spirit and (3) have wisdom.

The apostles were following Moses's example of distributing the workload by appointing men to help when he could not keep up with the needs of the Israelites while they were in the desert.

REFLECTIVE QUESTION: Am I using my gifts and talents by serving in my local church and/or in my community?

(Q) WHY WAS IT NECESSARY FOR THE APOSTLES TO ASSIGN RESPONSIBILITY FOR *"serving tables"* TO OTHER MEN?_____

(Q) WHY IS IT IMPORTANT TO HAVE REQUIREMENTS FOR CHURCH LEADERS?_____

(Q) ANY OTHER COMMENTS ON THESE VERSES?_____

STOP AND DISCUSS THE ABOVE VERSES AND QUESTIONS. **Answers to questions are on the next page.**

Answers to Questions from the Previous Page

(Q) Who Were the *native Hebrew widows*?

- They spoke the Hebrew language.
- They were very proud of their Jewish traditions.
- They lived in Jerusalem or around Jerusalem. In other words, they were local residents.

(Q) Who Were the *Hellenistic Jewish widows*?

- They were from different countries and traveled to Jerusalem for Pentecost.
- They did not speak Hebrew and spoke Greek because it was the most common language outside of Israel.
- In other words, they were in Jerusalem for Pentecost but were **not** locals.

(Q) Why Was It Necessary for the Apostles to Assign Responsibility for *"serving tables"* to Other Men?

- To free up the apostles to teach and preach.
- To divide the workload.
- To allow others to use their spiritual gifts and talents to serve God.

(Q) Why Is It Important to Have Requirements for Church Leaders?

- To confirm they have a proven track record and can handle managing God's resources and people.
- The requirements are outlined in Paul's first letter to Timothy:

An overseer, then, must be above reproach, the husband of one wife, temperate, self-controlled, respectable, hospitable, skillful in teaching, not overindulging in wine, not a bully, but gentle, not contentious, free from the love of money.

He must be one who manages his own household well, keeping his children under control with all dignity (but if a man does not know how to manage his own household, how will he take care of the church of God?), and not a new convert, so that he will not become conceited and fall into condemnation incurred by the devil.

And he must have a good reputation with those outside the church, so that he will not fall into disgrace and the snare of the devil. (1 Timothy 3:2–7)

> **Acts 6:5–8 (NASB).** [5] The announcement found approval with the whole congregation; and they chose Stephen, a man full of faith and of the Holy Spirit, and Philip, Prochorus, Nicanor, Timon, Parmenas, and Nicolas, a proselyte from Antioch.
> [6] And they brought these men before the apostles; and after praying, **they laid their hands on them**. [7] The word of God kept spreading; and the number of the disciples continued to increase greatly in Jerusalem, and a great many of the priests were becoming obedient to the faith. [8] And Stephen, full of grace and power, was performing great wonders and signs among the people.

Commentary. These verses signify the end of the first part of Acts, which described the **birth of the Christian church** in Jerusalem. The next three chapters describe *how* Stephen's selection as one of the first ministers in the church led to Christianity expanding into Samaria.

(Q) What Is the Meaning of Laying Hands on People?_____

(Q) Any Other Comments on These Verses?_____

STOP AND DISCUSS THE ABOVE VERSES AND QUESTIONS. Answers to questions are on the next page.

> **Acts 6:9–15 (NASB).** [9] But some men from what was called the **Synagogue of the Freedmen**, including both Cyrenians and Alexandrians, and some from Cilicia and Asia, rose up and argued with Stephen. [10] But they were unable to cope with his wisdom and the Spirit by whom he was speaking. [11] Then **they secretly induced men to say**,
> *"We have heard him speak blasphemous words against Moses and God."*
> [12] And they stirred up the people, the elders, and the scribes, and they came up to him and dragged him away, and brought him before the Council. [13] They put forward false witnesses who said,
> *"This man does not stop speaking against this holy place and the Law; [14] for we have heard him say that this Nazarene, Jesus, will destroy this place and change the customs which Moses handed down to us."*
> [15] And all who were sitting in the [Sanhedrin] Council stared at him, and **they saw his face, which was like the face of an angel.**

Commentary. The Synagogue of the Freedmen put up witnesses to falsely accuse Stephen of blasphemy. At his trial, God's glory was on Stephen, and his accusers saw the *"face of an angel."* The inference is that Stephen, like Moses and Jesus, was in the presence of the glory of God. The funny thing is, the Sadducees did not believe in angels. Tell me God doesn't have a sense of humor!

(Q) Who Were the *Synagogue of the Freedmen*?_____

(Q) Who Else Had a Radiant Face after Being in the Presence of the Lord?

_____

(Q) Any Other Comments on These Verses?_____

STOP AND DISCUSS THE ABOVE VERSES AND QUESTIONS. Answers to questions are on the next page.

(Q) What Is the Meaning of Laying Hands on People?

- The laying of hands has no power in and of itself. The power comes from the Holy Spirit through prayer that is done in agreement with God's Word.
- Prayer and laying of hands are commonly used when asking for healing, or blessing someone who is leaving the church on a missionary trip or relocating, or for someone who is assuming a leadership position in the church. There are other reasons, but these are the most common ones.
- In 1 Timothy, we are told, "*Do not be hasty in the laying on of hands, and do not share in the sins of others. Keep yourself pure*" (1 Timothy 5:22). This verse applies to appointing people to leadership positions in the church.

(Q) Who Were the *Synagogue of the Freedmen*?

- These men used to be slaves of the Romans who had been set free and became **proselytes**. A proselyte is a Gentile who has converted to Judaism.
- The NLT translation calls this group the **Synagogue of Freed Slaves**.

(Q) Who Else Had a Radiant Face after Being in the Presence of the Lord?

- Moses's face was radiant when he came down from Mount Sinai after being in the presence of the Lord. His face radiated so brightly that he had to wear a veil while speaking to the Israelites.

It came about, when Moses was coming down from Mount Sinai (and the two tablets of the testimony were in Moses' hand as he was coming down from the mountain), that Moses did not know that the skin of his face shone because of his speaking with Him. So when Aaron and all the sons of Israel saw Moses, behold, the skin of his face shone, and they were afraid to approach him.

Whenever he came out and spoke to the sons of Israel what he had been commanded, the sons of Israel would see the face of Moses, that the skin of Moses' face shone. So Moses would put the veil back over his face until he went in to speak with Him. (Exodus 34:29–30, 34–35)

Acts 7:1–8 (NASB). [1] Now the high priest said, *"Are these things so?"*
[2] And Stephen said,
"Listen to me, brothers and fathers! The God of glory appeared to our father Abraham when he was in Mesopotamia, before he lived in Haran, [3] *and He said to him,*
  'GO FROM YOUR COUNTRY AND YOUR RELATIVES,   **← Genesis 12:1**
  AND COME TO THE LAND WHICH I WILL SHOW YOU.'
[4] *Then he left the land of the Chaldeans and settled in Haran. And from there, after his father died, God had him move to this country in which you are now living.* [5] *But He gave him no inheritance in it, not even a foot of ground, and yet, He promised that He would give it to him as a possession, and to his descendants after him, even though he had no child.*
[6] *But* **God spoke** *to this effect, that his*
  'DESCENDANTS WOULD BE STRANGERS IN A LAND THAT WAS NOT THEIRS,   **← Genesis 15:13**
  AND THEY WOULD ENSLAVE AND MISTREAT THEM FOR FOUR HUNDRED YEARS.
  [7] AND WHATEVER NATION TO WHICH THEY ARE ENSLAVED I MYSELF WILL JUDGE,'
said God,
  'AND AFTER THAT THEY WILL COME OUT AND SERVE ME IN THIS PLACE.'
[8] *And* **He gave him the covenant of circumcision; and so, Abraham fathered Isaac,** *and circumcised him on the eighth day; and* **Isaac fathered Jacob, and Jacob, the twelve patriarchs.**"

Commentary. This is the beginning of **Stephen's defense** against the charge of blasphemy. He started his defense by talking about the father of our faith (Abraham), followed by Isaac, Jacob, and Joseph. He finished with Moses, David, Solomon and the Prophets.

Of course, the members of the Sanhedrin Council already knew about these men because they were experts in the Torah. Stephen was not just repeating Old Testament stories, he was proving that Jesus was the Messiah prophesized in the scriptures.

Throughout Stephen's defense, he repeatedly reminded the Sanhedrin of the *Jews' continuous rebellion, disobedience and idolatry.* In effect, Stephen's defense was using the Torah to accuse the members of the Sanhedrin Council of killing Jesus, the Messiah.

(Q) WHAT WAS THE *covenant of circumcision?*_____

(Q) WHO WERE THE *twelve patriarchs?*_____

(Q) ANY OTHER COMMENTS ON THESE VERSES?_____

STOP AND DISCUSS THE ABOVE VERSES AND QUESTIONS. Answers to questions are on the next page.

Next week we will finish Stephen's defense.

(Q) What Was the *covenant of circumcision*?

- A **covenant** is an agreement between two parties. In this case, it is an agreement between God and Abraham and his descendants. God told Abraham to leave his homeland, and then God made a covenant with Abraham that his descendants would be blessed and made into a great nation.

  Now the Lord said to Abram, "Go from your country, and from your relatives, and from your father's house, to the land which I will show you; and I will make you into a great nation, And I will bless you, and make your name great; and you shall be a blessing; and I will bless those who bless you, and the one who curses you I will curse. And in you all the families of the earth will be blessed." (Genesis 12:1–3)

- The **covenant of circumcision** is a sign of the covenant between God and Abraham.

  God said further to Abraham, "Now as for you, you shall keep My covenant, you and your descendants after you throughout their generations. This is My covenant, which you shall keep, between Me and you and your descendants after you: every male among you shall be circumcised. And you shall be circumcised in the flesh of your foreskin, and it shall be the sign of the covenant between Me and you." (Genesis 17:9–11)

(Q) Who Were the *twelve patriarchs*?

- This refers to the *twelve sons of Jacob*, also called the *twelve tribes of Israel*. God renamed Jacob to **Israel** after they wrestled all night (Genesis 32:28).
- Israel's twelve sons were

Reuben	Judah	Gad	Zebulun
Simeon	Dan	Asher	Joseph
Levi	Naphtali	Issachar	Benjamin

- Jesus came through the bloodline of Judah. Jesus's genealogy can be traced through His mother, **Mary**, all the way back to Adam and Eve (Luke 3:23–38).

Let's RE-Read Tonight's Verses

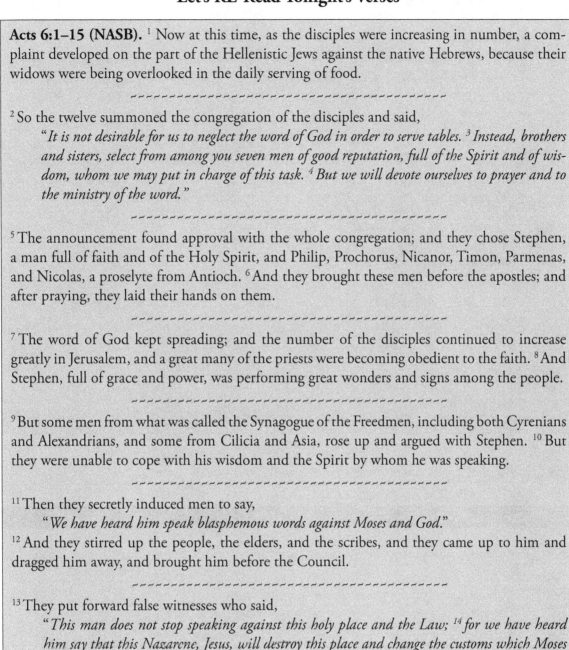

Acts 6:1–15 (NASB). [1] Now at this time, as the disciples were increasing in number, a complaint developed on the part of the Hellenistic Jews against the native Hebrews, because their widows were being overlooked in the daily serving of food.

- -

[2] So the twelve summoned the congregation of the disciples and said,
> *"It is not desirable for us to neglect the word of God in order to serve tables. [3] Instead, brothers and sisters, select from among you seven men of good reputation, full of the Spirit and of wisdom, whom we may put in charge of this task. [4] But we will devote ourselves to prayer and to the ministry of the word."*

- -

[5] The announcement found approval with the whole congregation; and they chose Stephen, a man full of faith and of the Holy Spirit, and Philip, Prochorus, Nicanor, Timon, Parmenas, and Nicolas, a proselyte from Antioch. [6] And they brought these men before the apostles; and after praying, they laid their hands on them.

- -

[7] The word of God kept spreading; and the number of the disciples continued to increase greatly in Jerusalem, and a great many of the priests were becoming obedient to the faith. [8] And Stephen, full of grace and power, was performing great wonders and signs among the people.

- -

[9] But some men from what was called the Synagogue of the Freedmen, including both Cyrenians and Alexandrians, and some from Cilicia and Asia, rose up and argued with Stephen. [10] But they were unable to cope with his wisdom and the Spirit by whom he was speaking.

- -

[11] Then they secretly induced men to say,
> *"We have heard him speak blasphemous words against Moses and God."*

[12] And they stirred up the people, the elders, and the scribes, and they came up to him and dragged him away, and brought him before the Council.

- -

[13] They put forward false witnesses who said,
> *"This man does not stop speaking against this holy place and the Law; [14] for we have heard him say that this Nazarene, Jesus, will destroy this place and change the customs which Moses handed down to us."*

[15] And all who were sitting in the Council stared at him, and they saw his face, which was like the face of an angel.

- -

Acts 7:1–8 (NASB). [1] Now the high priest said,

> *"Are these things so?"*

[2] And Stephen said,

> *"Listen to me, brothers and fathers! The God of glory appeared to our father Abraham when he was in Mesopotamia, before he lived in Haran,* [3] *and He said to him,*
>
> *'Go from your country and your relatives, and come to the land which I will show you.'"*

- -

> [4] *"Then he left the land of the Chaldeans and settled in Haran. And from there, after his father died, God had him move to this country in which you are now living.* [5] *But He gave him no inheritance in it, not even a foot of ground, and yet, He promised that He would give it to him as a possession, and to his descendants after him, even though he had no child."*

- -

> [6] *"But God spoke to this effect, that his*
>
> *'descendants would be strangers in a land that was not theirs, and they would enslave and mistreat them for four hundred years.* [7] *And whatever nation to which they are enslaved I Myself will judge,'"*

- -

> *"said God,*
>
> *'And after that they will come out and serve Me in this place.'* [8] *And He gave him the covenant of circumcision; and so Abraham fathered Isaac, and circumcised him on the eighth day; and Isaac fathered Jacob, and Jacob, the twelve patriarchs."*

(Q) Any Final Comments?_____

This is the end of this week's study.

A Precept Bible Study

ACTS

The Birth of the Church

Week 7, Acts 7:8–60

A Verse-by-Verse Journey through the book of Acts

Let's Review Last Week's Study

The early church members voluntarily gave their wealth and possessions to the apostles, who in turn redistributed the goods to the congregation (Christian socialism as opposed to political socialism).

A problem in the church occurred when the people complained that the apostles were taking care of the native Jewish widows and not the Hellenistic Jewish widows. The apostles' solution was to appoint seven men of good reputation to serve the people. Stephen was one of the men selected, making him one of the first ministers in the church. Shortly after being selected, Stephen was falsely accused of blasphemy by the Synagogue of the Freedmen and brought to trial in front of the Sanhedrin Council. Stephen started his defense with a summary of how God made a covenant with Abraham.

(Q) ANY OTHER COMMENTS ON CHAPTER 6?_____

STOP AND DISCUSS THE ABOVE COMMENTS.

Let's Begin Tonight's Study

> **Acts 7:8–16 (NASB).** [Stephen said] [8] *"He gave him the covenant of circumcision; and so, Abraham fathered Isaac, and circumcised him on the eighth day; and Isaac fathered Jacob, and Jacob [fathered the] the twelve patriarchs. [9] The patriarchs became jealous of Joseph and sold him into Egypt. Yet God was with him, [10] and rescued him from all his afflictions, and granted him favor and wisdom in the sight of Pharaoh, king of Egypt, and he made him governor over Egypt and his entire household.*
> [11] *Now a famine came over all Egypt and Canaan, and great affliction with it, and our fathers could find no food. [12] But when Jacob heard that there was grain in Egypt, he sent our fathers there the first time. [13] And on the second visit, Joseph made himself known to his brothers, and Joseph's family was revealed to Pharaoh. [14] Then Joseph sent word and invited his father Jacob and all his relatives to come to him, seventy-five people in all. [15] And Jacob went down to Egypt, and he and our fathers died there. [16] And they were brought back from there to Shechem and laid in the tomb which Abraham had purchased for a sum of money from the sons of Hamor in Shechem."*

Commentary. Stephen continued his defense against the charge of blasphemy by reminding the Sanhedrin of how their forefathers ended up in Egypt, and that God was with them no matter where they lived.

Verse 12 is a little confusing because Stephen said, "*Jacob sent our fathers*" rather than saying, "*Jacob sent his sons.*" The reason Stephen referred to Jacob's sons as "*our fathers*" was because Stephen was referring to Jacob's sons from his own perspective.

(Q) WHAT DO YOU KNOW ABOUT JACOB?_____

(Q) WHAT DO YOU KNOW ABOUT JOSEPH, SON OF JACOB?_____

(Q) ANY COMMENTS ON THESE VERSES?_____

STOP AND DISCUSS THE ABOVE VERSES AND QUESTIONS. Answers to questions are on the next page.

Answers to Questions from the Previous Page

(Q) What Do You Know about Jacob?

- His mother was Rebekah and his father was Isaac.
- He was a twin and was born clutching his brother Esau's heel.
- Jacob's name means "*he deceives.*"
- During Rebekah's pregnancy, God told her there were twins in her womb that were fighting, and her sons would lead two nations that would be at war their entire lives.
- Near the end of Isaacs's life, he called for Esau so he could give him his blessing, but Rebekah devised a plan to trick Isaac into giving his blessing to Jacob.
- Jacob wrestled all night with God until God touched Jacob's hip, putting it out of socket. At daybreak, Jacob refused to let go, and asked for a blessing. God responded with, "*Your name will no longer be Jacob, but Israel, because you have struggled with God*" (Genesis 32:28).
- Israel's sons and grandsons became the twelve patriarchs, also called the twelve tribes of Israel.

(Q) What Do You Know about Joseph, Son of Jacob?

- His father was Jacob and his mother was Rachel (Genesis 35:23–24).
- Jacob loved Joseph more than any of his other sons because he had him in his old age (Genesis 37:3).
- Joseph's brothers were *jealous* of him.
- Joseph told his brothers that he had a dream that he would rule over them (Genesis 37:9–10).
- Joseph's brothers hated him so much, they sold him into slavery and then convinced their father that he was eaten by wild animals (Genesis 37:27–28).
- The merchants sold Joseph to a high-ranking Egyptian named Potiphar (Genesis 39:1).
- Potiphar's wife falsely accused Joseph of trying to sleep with her (Genesis 39:11–18).
- Joseph worked hard and eventually became the supervisor of Potiphar's household.
- Pharaoh asked Joseph to interpret his dreams (Genesis 41:14–15).
- Based on Pharaoh's dreams, Joseph predicted seven years of plentiful harvests followed by seven years of famine. Then Joseph warned Pharaoh to store grain in preparation for the coming drought (Genesis 41:16–32).
- For his wisdom, Joseph was put in charge of the whole land of Egypt and was second-in-command only to Pharaoh (Genesis 41:38–43).
- Jacob heard that there was food in Egypt and sent his sons to buy food (Genesis 42:1–5).
- Eventually, Joseph forgave his brothers and called for his father and the rest of the Israelites to come to Egypt, where they stayed for the next four hundred years (Genesis 45:1–15).

Acts 7:17–29 (NASB). ¹⁷ *"But as the time of the promise which God had assured to Abraham was approaching, the people increased and multiplied in Egypt,* ¹⁸ *until*

> *'ANOTHER KING AROSE OVER EGYPT WHO*
> *DID NOT KNOW JOSEPH.'*   ← *Exodus 1:8*

¹⁹ *It was he who shrewdly took advantage of our nation and mistreated our fathers in order that they would abandon their infants in the Nile, so that they would not survive.* ²⁰ *At this time Moses was born; and he was beautiful to God. He was nurtured for three months in his father's home.* ²¹ *And after he had been put outside, Pharaoh's daughter took him away and nurtured him as her own son.* ²² *Moses was educated in all the wisdom of the Egyptians, and he was proficient in speaking and action.*

²³ *But when he was approaching the age of forty, it entered his mind to visit his countrymen, the sons of Israel.* ²⁴ *And when he saw one of them being treated unjustly, he defended and took vengeance for the oppressed man by fatally striking the Egyptian.* ²⁵ *And he thought that his brothers understood that God was granting them deliverance through him; but they did not understand.* ²⁶ *And on the following day he appeared to them as they were fighting each other, and he tried to reconcile them to peace, by saying,*

> *'Men, you are brothers, why are you injuring each other?'*

²⁷ *But the one who was injuring his neighbor pushed him away, saying,*

> *'WHO MADE YOU A RULER AND JUDGE OVER US?*   ← *Exodus 2:14*
> ²⁸ *YOU DO NOT INTEND TO KILL ME AS YOU KILLED THE*
> *EGYPTIAN YESTERDAY, DO YOU?'*

²⁹ *At this remark, MOSES FLED AND BECAME A STRANGER IN THE LAND OF MIDIAN, where he fathered two sons."*

Commentary. Stephen quoted the Torah to show *how* the Israelites became slaves in Egypt after a new king arose (v. 17–19). Since Stephen was being *accused of talking against Moses*, he wanted to show that he admired Moses and that it was the Jewish forefathers who rejected Moses.

In verse 25, Moses believed he was called by God to deliver his people; however, the people did not understand or believe him. Consequently, Moses went into the desert for forty years before fulfilling God's calling for his life.

OUR LESSON: Is God calling me for a particular ministry, but resistance from others has discouraged me, and I have given up? Or is fear stopping me from moving forward?

(Q) WHAT DO WE KNOW ABOUT MOSES?_____

(Q) ANY COMMENTS ON THESE VERSES?_____

STOP AND DISCUSS THE ABOVE VERSES AND QUESTIONS. **Answers to questions are on the next page.**

ANSWERS TO QUESTION FROM THE PREVIOUS PAGE

(Q) WHAT DO WE KNOW ABOUT MOSES?

- We met Moses when Pharaoh ordered the death of all the male Hebrew children. Moses's mother placed him in a basket and put him in the Nile River to save him from certain death (Exodus 1:22).
- The basket was found by Pharaoh's daughter and she adopted Moses and raised him in Pharaoh's palace.
- As an adult, Moses killed a Hebrew while breaking up a fight and then panicked and fled Egypt (Exodus 2:14).
- After living in Midian for forty years, God called Moses to lead the Israelites out of captivity in Egypt to the promised land.
- Pharaoh refused to let the Israelites go, so God's judgment fell on the Egyptians in the form of ten plagues. The final plague was the slaying of the firstborn (Passover).
- After the exodus, Moses led the Hebrews to the edge of the Red Sea, where God provided another miracle by parting the waters and allowing the Hebrews to pass to the other side while drowning the Egyptian army (Exodus 14).
- Moses brought the people to the foot of Mount Sinai where **God gave him the Ten Commandments** and the Old Covenant was established between God and the newly formed nation of Israel (Exodus 19–24).
- Moses had a stuttering problem (Exodus 4:10).
- Moses had a brother named Aaron.

Acts 7:30–38 (NASB). ³⁰ *"After forty years had passed, an angel appeared to Moses in the wilderness of Mount Sinai, in the flame of a burning thorn bush.* ³¹ *When Moses saw it, he was astonished at the sight; and as he approached to look more closely, the voice of the Lord came:*

³² '*I AM THE GOD OF YOUR FATHERS,*   ← **Exodus 3:6**
       THE GOD OF ABRAHAM, AND ISAAC, AND JACOB.'

Moses shook with fear and did not dare to look closely. ³³ *But the LORD said to him,*

'*REMOVE YOUR SANDALS FROM YOUR FEET,*   ← **Exodus 3:5–8**
FOR THE PLACE ON WHICH YOU ARE STANDING IS HOLY GROUND.
³⁴ *I HAVE CERTAINLY SEEN THE OPPRESSION OF MY PEOPLE WHO ARE IN EGYPT,*
AND HAVE HEARD THEIR GROANING, AND I HAVE COME DOWN TO RESCUE THEM;
AND NOW COME, I WILL SEND YOU TO EGYPT.'

³⁵ *This Moses whom they disowned, saying,*

'*WHO MADE YOU A RULER AND A JUDGE?'*   ← **Exodus 2:14**

is the one whom God sent to be both a ruler and a deliverer with the help of the angel who appeared to him in the thorn bush. ³⁶ *This man led them out, performing wonders and signs in the land of Egypt and in the Red Sea, and in the wilderness for forty years.* ³⁷ *This is the Moses who said to the sons of Israel,*

'*GOD WILL RAISE UP FOR YOU A PROPHET LIKE ME*
FROM YOUR COUNTRYMEN.'   ← **Deuteronomy 18:15**

³⁸ *This is the one who was in the assembly in the wilderness together with the angel who spoke to him at length on Mount Sinai, and who was with our fathers; and he received living words to pass on to you."*

Commentary. Stephen continued his account of Moses life by intertwining quotes from the Old Testament with his own narration. He emphasized that the Israelites once again disowned and rejected the man whom God sent to deliver them. First, they rejected Joseph and now Moses. We will see later that the Israelites rejected Moses a second time.

(Q) WHAT SIGNS AND WONDERS DOES VERSE 36 REFER TO?_____

(Q) WHAT DOES VERSE 37 MEAN, "GOD WILL RAISE UP FOR YOU A PROPHET"?

_____

(Q) WHAT DOES VERSE 38b MEAN, "He received living words to pass on to you"?

_____

(Q) ANY COMMENTS ON THESE VERSES?_____

STOP AND DISCUSS THE ABOVE VERSES AND QUESTIONS. **Answers to questions are on the next page.**

ANSWERS TO QUESTIONS FROM THE PREVIOUS PAGE

(Q) WHAT SIGNS AND WONDERS DOES VERSE 36 REFER TO?

- The ten plagues on Egypt (Exodus 8).

    1. The water in the Nile River turned into blood.
    2. A swarm of frogs came from the Nile River and invaded Egypt.
    3. A swarm of gnats invaded Egypt.
    4. A swarm of flies invaded Egypt.
    5. The Egyptians' livestock perished, but the Israelites' livestock was spared.
    6. The Egyptians were plagued with boils.
    7. Hail rained down from the heavens, and fire ran across the land.
    8. A swarm of locust invaded Egypt and ate their crops.
    9. Egypt was covered with darkness for three days.
    10. The angel of death brought death to the firstborn Egyptian males

- Moses parted the Red Sea (Exodus 14).

(Q) WHAT DOES VERSE 37 MEAN, *"GOD WILL RAISE UP FOR YOU A PROPHET"*?

- Jesus Christ

(Q) WHAT DOES VERSE 38b MEAN, *"He received living words to pass on to you"*?

- The Ten Commandments

> **Acts 7:39–43 (NASB).** ³⁹ *"Our fathers were unwilling to be obedient to [Moses]; on the contrary they rejected him and turned back to Egypt in their hearts,* ⁴⁰ *saying to Aaron,*
>
>   *'Make Us a God Who Will Go before Us;*   ← *Exodus 32:23*
>   *for This Moses Who Led Us Out of the Land of Egypt,*
>   *We Do Not Know What Happened to Him.'*
>
> ⁴¹ *At that time they made a calf and brought a sacrifice to the idol, and were rejoicing in the works of their hands.* ⁴² *But **God turned away and gave them over to serve the heavenly lights**; as it is written in the book of the prophets:*
>
>   *'You Did Not Offer Me Victims and Sacrifices*   ← *Amos 5:24–26*
>   *for Forty Years in the Wilderness, Did You,*
>   *House of Israel?* ⁴³ *You Also Took Along*
>   *the Tabernacle of Moloch*
>   *and the Star of Your God Rompha,*
>   *the Images Which You Made to Worship.*
>   *I Also Will Deport You beyond Babylon."*

Commentary. Stephen emphasized that their Jewish ancestors disowned, rejected and disobeyed Moses *again* and they even asked Aaron to make them a false idol to worship. God allowed them to do whatever they wanted and as a result of their disobedience and idolatry, God turned away from them.

(Q) What Do We Know about Aaron? _____

(Q) In Verse 42, What Does "*heavenly lights*" Mean? _____

(Q) Any Comments on These Verses? _____

Stop and Discuss the Above Verses and Questions. Answers to questions are on the next page.

> **Acts 7:44–45 (NASB).** ⁴⁴ *"Our fathers had the **tabernacle of testimony in the wilderness**, just as He who spoke to Moses directed him to make it according to the pattern which he had seen.* ⁴⁵ *Our fathers in turn received it, and they also brought it in with Joshua upon dispossessing the nations that God drove out from our fathers, until the time of David."*

Commentary. In these verses, Stephen described when Joshua led the Israelites into the promised land and God gave them victory over the Canaanites, which fulfilled the promise God made to the Israelites (Genesis 15:18–20).

(Q) In Verse 44, What Does the "*tabernacle of testimony in the wilderness*" Mean?

_____

(Q) What Do We Know about Joshua? _____

(Q) Any Comments on These Verses? _____

Stop and Discuss the Above Verses and Questions. Answers to questions are on the next page.

Answers to Questions from the Previous Page

(Q) What Do We Know about Aaron?

- He was Moses's brother.
- Aaron went to Egypt with Moses to free the Israelites from Pharaoh.
- Since Moses had a stuttering problem, Aaron often acted as Moses's spokesman (Exodus 4:10, Exodus 7:1–6).

(Q) In Verse 42, What Does "*heavenly lights*" Mean?

- Refers to the Israelites worshipping the stars in the sky.
- In today's world, this would be like people who worship astrology and zodiac signs.
- In other words, it refers to people who worship false idols.

(Q) In Verse 44, What Does the "*tabernacle of testimony in the wilderness*" mean?

- Refers to the **ark of the covenant** (Exodus 25:10).
- The ark was to be a place for God to dwell (Exodus 25:8–9).
- God gave specific instructions on how to build the ark (Exodus 25:21–22).
- The ark housed the tablets with the Ten Commandments given to Moses.
- No one was allowed to touch the ark, or they would die (Numbers 4:15).

(Q) What Do We Know about Joshua?

- He is best known as Moses's second-in-command.
- He led the Israelites into the promised land after Moses's death (Deuteronomy 34).
- He is considered one of the Bible's greatest military leaders for leading the seven-year conquest of the promised land.
- He is considered one of the Bible's greatest leaders and many people today still model his leadership style.
- The book of Joshua has one of the most quoted Bible verses:

Choose this day whom you will serve, as for me and my house, we will serve the Lord. (Joshua 24:15)

> **Acts 7:46–50 (NASB).** ⁴⁶ *"David found favor in God's sight, and asked that he might find a dwelling place for the house of Jacob.* ⁴⁷ *But it was Solomon who built a house for Him.* ⁴⁸ *However,* **the Most High does not dwell in houses made by human hands***; as the prophet says:*
> ⁴⁹ *'HEAVEN IS MY THRONE,*   ← *Isaiah 66:1*
>   *AND THE EARTH IS THE FOOTSTOOL OF MY FEET;*
>   *WHAT KIND OF HOUSE WILL YOU BUILD FOR ME?' says the Lord,*
>   *'OR WHAT PLACE IS THERE FOR MY REST?*   ← *Isaiah 66:2*
> ⁵⁰ *WAS IT NOT MY HAND THAT MADE ALL THESE THINGS?"*

Commentary. Stephen continued his defense by talking about David's desire to build a temple for God, and then he made a huge declaration: *"God does not dwell in houses made by human hands."* Stephen supported his claim by quoting Isaiah 66:1–2, which said *"Heaven was God's throne"* and the *"earth was the Lord's footstool."* Stephen continued by asking two questions: (1) what kind of house could man possibly build for the Creator of the universe and (2) was it not the Lord's hand that made all these things? This angered the Sanhedrin because the Law and the temple were very important to them, and Stephen just told them that God did not need a house made by human hands.

(Q) WHAT DO WE KNOW ABOUT DAVID?_____

(Q) WHAT DO WE KNOW ABOUT SOLOMON?_____

(Q) ANY COMMENTS ON THESE VERSES?_____

STOP AND DISCUSS THE ABOVE VERSES AND QUESTIONS. Answers to questions are on the next page.

> **Acts 7:51–53 (NASB).** ⁵¹ *"**You men who are stiff-necked and uncircumcised in heart and ears are always resisting the Holy Spirit***; you are doing just as your fathers did.* ⁵² *Which one of the prophets did your fathers not persecute? They killed those who had previously announced the coming of the Righteous One, and you have now become betrayers and murderers of Him;* ⁵³ *you who received the Law as ordained by angels, and yet did not keep it."*

Commentary. Stephen finished his defense with a bang. So far, he has used the Torah to prove their Jewish ancestors disobeyed God over and over and made false idols and rejected all the men that God sent to deliver the Israelites. And now Stephen accused the Sadducees and Pharisees of doing the same thing as their forefathers when they killed Jesus.

   If you do not believe God has a sense of humor, reread verse 52a with attitude!

(Q) WHAT DOES *"uncircumcised in heart"* MEAN?_____

(Q) ANY COMMENTS ON THESE VERSES?_____

STOP AND DISCUSS THE ABOVE VERSES AND QUESTIONS. Answers to questions are on the next page.

(Q) WHAT DO WE KNOW ABOUT DAVID?

- He was a shepherd boy and was Jesse's youngest son (1 Samuel 16:10).
- He killed Goliath with just a slingshot and a smooth stone (1 Samuel 17:45–46).
- God told Samuel to appoint David as the second king of Israel (1 Samuel 16:13).
- He became one of King Saul's armor-bearers (1 Samuel 16:21).
- He was best friends with Jonathon, who was King Saul's son (1 Samuel 18:1–4, 19–20).
- He was a great military leader and led Israel into many battles (1 Samuel 4).
- He had many wives (1 Samuel 25:43–44).
- After he became king, he brought the ark of the covenant back to Israel (2 Samuel 6:1–7, 11–16).
- He was known as *a man after God's own heart* (Acts 13:22).
- He had an affair with Bathsheba and got her pregnant (2 Samuel 11).
- Then he had her husband, Uriah, killed to cover up the affair (2 Samuel 11:14–21).
- God sent Nathan the Prophet to confront David (2 Samuel 11).
- David wrote many of the Psalms and was called *"the sweet Psalmist of Israel"* (2 Samuel 23:1).
- God promised David that the Messiah would come through his bloodline (2 Samuel 7:4–17).
- David and Bathsheba had another son named Solomon (2 Samuel 12:24).

(Q) WHAT DO WE KNOW ABOUT SOLOMON?

- He was the son of David and Bathsheba and became the third king over Israel (Ecclesiastes 1:1).
- He built the temple that his father David wanted to build (Chronicles 22).
- He wrote *Ecclesiastes*, *Song of Songs* and many of the *Proverbs*.
- He prayed for wisdom and was known as the wisest man alive (1 Kings 10:23).

(Q) WHAT DOES *"uncircumcised in heart"* MEAN?

- Jewish circumcision is an outward sign of being set apart to God.
- However, physical circumcision cannot make a person right with God if the heart is sinful.
- True circumcision is a matter of the heart and is performed by the Holy Spirit.

Circumcise yourselves to the LORD, and remove the foreskins of your hearts. (Jeremiah 4:4)

The LORD your God will circumcise your heart and the hearts of your descendants, to love the LORD your God with all your heart and all your soul. (Deuteronomy 30:6)

> **Acts 7:54–60 (NASB).** ⁵⁴ Now when the [Sadducees and Pharisees] heard this, they were infuriated, and they began gnashing their teeth at him. ⁵⁵ But **[Stephen], being full of the Holy Spirit, looked intently into heaven and saw the glory of God, and Jesus standing at the right hand of God**; ⁵⁶ and he said,
> *"Behold, I see the heavens opened and the Son of Man standing at the right hand of God."*
> ⁵⁷ But they shouted with loud voices, and covered their ears and rushed at him with one mind. ⁵⁸ When they had driven him out of the city, they began stoning him; and the witnesses laid aside their cloaks at the feet of a young man named Saul. ⁵⁹ They went on stoning Stephen as he called on the Lord and said,
> *"Lord Jesus, receive my spirit!"*
> ⁶⁰ Then he fell on his knees and cried out with a loud voice,
> *"Lord, do not hold this sin against them!"*
> Having said this, he fell asleep.

Commentary. When Stephen looked into heaven and saw where Jesus dwells, he was more than likely looking into the **third heaven** that Paul described in second Corinthians.

> *I know a man in Christ, who fourteen years ago—whether in the body I do not know, or out of the body I do not know, God knows—such a man was **caught up to the third heaven**. And I know how such a man—whether in the body or apart from the body I do not know, God knows—was **caught up into Paradise** and heard inexpressible words, which a man is not permitted to speak (2 Corinthians 12:2–4; emphasis added).*

By referring to Jesus as *"standing at the right hand of God,"* Stephen was saying that Jesus has the same authority as God. This infuriated the Jews so much that they covered their ears and then they stoned him to death. **Stephen became the first martyr** and died a painful death, but he was calm and did not speak unkind words against his attackers. In fact, he asked God not to hold their sin against them, *wow*!

OUR LESSON: Lord, may I have the same attitude toward my enemies as Stephen had toward the people who stoned him to death.

(Q) WHY IS JESUS REFERRED TO AS THE *"SON OF MAN"*?_____

(Q) WHAT IS THE THIRD HEAVEN?_____

(Q) ANY COMMENTS ON THESE VERSES?_____

STOP AND DISCUSS THE ABOVE VERSES AND QUESTIONS. Answers to questions are on the next page.

Note: This is the first mention of Saul of Tarsus. Next week, we will read more about Saul in chapter 8.

(Q) WHY IS JESUS REFERRED TO AS THE "SON OF MAN"?

- Jesus is called the "*Son of Man*" eighty-eight times in the New Testament.
- The "*Son of Man*" referred to the prophecies in Daniel about the Messiah.
  - Daniel 7:13–14 says, "*Behold, with the clouds of heaven, One like a **son of man** was coming, and He came up to the Ancient of Days, and was presented before Him. And to Him was given dominion, Honor, and a kingdom, so that all the peoples, nations, and populations of all languages Might serve Him.*"
  - When Jesus used this phrase, He was assigning the "*Son of Man*" prophecies to Himself.
  - In other words, Jesus was proclaiming Himself as the Messiah.
- A second meaning of the phrase "*Son of Man*" is that
  - Jesus was fully God (John 1:1).
  - Jesus was also fully human (John 1:14).

(Q) WHAT IS THE THIRD HEAVEN?

If there is a third heaven, then there must be a first and second heaven, *right*?

- The first heaven is the PHYSICAL REALM such as the earth, sun, moon, stars (Genesis 22:17, Revelations 21:1).
- The second heaven is the SPIRITUAL REALM where the angels and demons reside.
- The third heaven is the SPIRITUAL HEAVEN where God resides (2 Corinthians 12:2–4).
- So when Paul and Stephen mentioned the third heaven, they were saying they were in the presence of God, and His glory shown on their faces!

Let's RE-Read Tonight's Verses

Acts 7:1–60 (NASB). [1] Now the high priest said,
"Are these things so?"
[2] And Stephen said,

> "*Listen to me, brothers and fathers! The God of glory appeared to our father Abraham when he was in Mesopotamia, before he lived in Haran,* [3] *and He said to him,*
> '*GO FROM YOUR COUNTRY AND YOUR RELATIVES, AND COME TO THE LAND WHICH I WILL SHOW YOU.*'"

> [4] "*Then he left the land of the Chaldeans and settled in Haran. And from there, after his father died, God had him move to this country in which you are now living.* [5] *But He gave him no inheritance in it, not even a foot of ground, and yet, He promised that He would give it to him as a possession, and to his descendants after him, even though he had no child.*"

> [6] "*But God spoke to this effect, that his*
> '*DESCENDANTS WOULD BE STRANGERS IN A LAND THAT WAS NOT THEIRS,*
> *AND THEY WOULD ENSLAVE AND MISTREAT THEM FOR FOUR HUNDRED YEARS.*
> [7] *AND WHATEVER NATION TO WHICH THEY ARE ENSLAVED I MYSELF WILL JUDGE,*'
> *said God,*
> '*AND AFTER THAT THEY WILL COME OUT AND SERVE ME IN THIS PLACE.*'"

> [8] "*And He gave him the covenant of circumcision; and so Abraham fathered Isaac, and circumcised him on the eighth day; and Isaac fathered Jacob, and Jacob, the twelve patriarchs.* [9] *The patriarchs became jealous of Joseph and sold him into Egypt. Yet God was with him,* [10] *and rescued him from all his afflictions, and granted him favor and wisdom in the sight of Pharaoh, king of Egypt, and he made him governor over Egypt and his entire household.*"

> [11] "*Now a famine came over all Egypt and Canaan, and great affliction with it, and our fathers could find no food.* [12] *But when Jacob heard that there was grain in Egypt, he sent our fathers there the first time.* [13] *And on the second visit, Joseph made himself known to his brothers, and Joseph's family was revealed to Pharaoh.* [14] *Then Joseph sent word and invited his father Jacob and all his relatives to come to him, seventy-five people in all.*"

> [15] "*And Jacob went down to Egypt, and he and our fathers died there.* [16] *And they were brought back from there to Shechem and laid in the tomb which Abraham had purchased for a sum of money from the sons of Hamor in Shechem.*"

----

[17] "But as the time of the promise which God had assured to Abraham was approaching, the people increased and multiplied in Egypt,

[18] 'until ANOTHER KING AROSE OVER EGYPT WHO DID NOT KNOW JOSEPH.'

[19] It was he who shrewdly took advantage of our nation and mistreated our fathers in order that they would abandon their infants in the Nile, so that they would not survive."

- -

[20] "At this time Moses was born; and he was beautiful to God. He was nurtured for three months in his father's home. [21] And after he had been put outside, Pharaoh's daughter took him away and nurtured him as her own son. [22] Moses was educated in all the wisdom of the Egyptians, and he was proficient in speaking and action."

- -

[23] "But when he was approaching the age of forty, it entered his mind to visit his countrymen, the sons of Israel. [24] And when he saw one of them being treated unjustly, he defended and took vengeance for the oppressed man by fatally striking the Egyptian. [25] And he thought that his brothers understood that God was granting them deliverance through him; but they did not understand."

- -

[26] "And on the following day he appeared to them as they were fighting each other, and he tried to reconcile them to peace, by saying,

'Men, you are brothers, why are you injuring each other?'

[27] But the one who was injuring his neighbor pushed him away, saying,

'WHO MADE YOU A RULER AND JUDGE OVER US?

[28] YOU DO NOT INTEND TO KILL ME AS YOU KILLED THE EGYPTIAN YESTERDAY, DO YOU?'"

- -

[29] "At this remark, MOSES FLED AND BECAME A STRANGER IN THE LAND OF MIDIAN, where he fathered two sons. [30] After forty years had passed, an angel appeared to him in the wilderness of Mount Sinai, in the flame of a burning thorn bush. [31] When Moses saw it, he was astonished at the sight; and as he approached to look more closely, the voice of the Lord came:

[32] 'I AM THE GOD OF YOUR FATHERS, THE GOD OF ABRAHAM, AND ISAAC, AND JACOB.'"

- -

"Moses shook with fear and did not dare to look closely. [33] But the LORD said to him,

'REMOVE YOUR SANDALS FROM YOUR FEET,

FOR THE PLACE ON WHICH YOU ARE STANDING IS HOLY GROUND.

[34] I HAVE CERTAINLY SEEN THE OPPRESSION OF MY PEOPLE WHO ARE IN EGYPT,

AND HAVE HEARD THEIR GROANING,

AND I HAVE COME DOWN TO RESCUE THEM;

AND NOW COME, I WILL SEND YOU TO EGYPT.'"

- -

³⁵ "This Moses whom they disowned, saying,

'WHO MADE YOU A RULER AND A JUDGE?'

is the one whom God sent to be both a ruler and a deliverer with the help of the angel who appeared to him in the thorn bush. ³⁶ This man led them out, performing wonders and signs in the land of Egypt and in the Red Sea, and in the wilderness for forty years."

----

³⁷ "This is the Moses who said to the sons of Israel,

'GOD WILL RAISE UP FOR YOU A PROPHET LIKE ME FROM YOUR COUNTRYMEN.'

³⁸ This is the one who was in the assembly in the wilderness together with the angel who spoke to him at length on Mount Sinai, and who was with our fathers; and he received living words to pass on to you."

----

³⁹ "Our fathers were unwilling to be obedient to Him; on the contrary they rejected Him and turned back to Egypt in their hearts, ⁴⁰ saying to Aaron,

'MAKE US A GOD WHO WILL GO BEFORE US;

FOR THIS MOSES WHO LED US OUT OF THE LAND OF EGYPT

WE DO NOT KNOW WHAT HAPPENED TO HIM.'

⁴¹ At that time they made a calf and brought a sacrifice to the idol, and were rejoicing in the works of their hands."

----

⁴² "But God turned away and gave them over to serve the heavenly lights; as it is written in the book of the prophets:

'YOU DID NOT OFFER ME VICTIMS AND SACRIFICES FOR FORTY YEARS IN THE WILDERNESS, DID YOU, HOUSE OF ISRAEL? ⁴³ YOU ALSO TOOK ALONG THE TABERNACLE OF MOLOCH AND THE STAR OF YOUR GOD ROMPHA, THE IMAGES WHICH YOU MADE TO WORSHIP. I ALSO WILL DEPORT YOU BEYOND BABYLON.'"

----

⁴⁴ "Our fathers had the tabernacle of testimony in the wilderness, just as He who spoke to Moses directed him to make it according to the pattern which he had seen. ⁴⁵ Our fathers in turn received it, and they also brought it in with Joshua upon dispossessing the nations that God drove out from our fathers, until the time of David. ⁴⁶ David found favor in God's sight, and asked that he might find a dwelling place for the house of Jacob. ⁴⁷ But it was Solomon who built a house for Him."

----

⁴⁸ "However, the Most High does not dwell in houses made by human hands; as the prophet says:

⁴⁹ 'HEAVEN IS MY THRONE,

AND THE EARTH IS THE FOOTSTOOL OF MY FEET;

WHAT KIND OF HOUSE WILL YOU BUILD FOR ME?'"

"says the Lord,
'OR WHAT PLACE IS THERE FOR MY REST?
⁵⁰ WAS IT NOT MY HAND THAT MADE ALL THESE THINGS?'"

⁵¹ "You men who are stiff-necked and uncircumcised in heart and ears are always resisting the Holy Spirit; you are doing just as your fathers did. ⁵² Which one of the prophets did your fathers not persecute? They killed those who had previously announced the coming of the Righteous One, and you have now become betrayers and murderers of Him; ⁵³ you who received the Law as ordained by angels, and yet did not keep it."

~~~~~~

⁵⁴ Now when they heard this, they were infuriated, and they began gnashing their teeth at him. ⁵⁵ But he, being full of the Holy Spirit, looked intently into heaven and saw the glory of God, and Jesus standing at the right hand of God; ⁵⁶ and he said,
"Behold, I see the heavens opened and the Son of Man standing at the right hand of God."
⁵⁷ But they shouted with loud voices, and covered their ears and rushed at him with one mind.

~~~~~~

⁵⁸ When they had driven him out of the city, they began stoning him; and the witnesses laid aside their cloaks at the feet of a young man named Saul. ⁵⁹ They went on stoning Stephen as he called on the Lord and said,
"Lord Jesus, receive my spirit!"
⁶⁰ Then he fell on his knees and cried out with a loud voice,
"Lord, do not hold this sin against them!"
Having said this, he fell asleep.

(Q) ANY FINAL COMMENTS?_____

THIS IS THE END OF THIS WEEK'S STUDY.

A Precept Bible Study

ACTS

The Birth of the Church

Week 8, Acts 8:1–40

A Verse-by-Verse Journey through the book of Acts

Let's Review Last Week's Study

- Stephen was chosen to help the apostles serve the people and was one of the first church ministers.
- A group of proselytes called the Synagogue of the Freedmen were jealous of Stephen and falsely accused him of blasphemy and brought him to trial in front of the Sanhedrin Council.
- Stephen began his defense by discussing the covenant of circumcision that God made with Abraham to show the Israelites how special the Jewish people were to God.
- Then he gave examples of the Israelites' rebellion against God and their idolatry of handmade idols. He also pointed out that each time God sent someone to deliver the Israelites, they rejected him, and when Jesus came, they crucified Him.
- Stephen finished his defense by calling the Sanhedrin Council *stiff-necked and uncircumcised in heart* and accused them of "*doing just as their fathers did.*"
- After Stephen finished, they ran him out of town and stoned him to death. As Stephen fell to his knees, he cried out, "*Lord, do not hold this sin against them!*" And then he fell asleep.

(Q) Any Other Comments on Chapter 7?_____

Stop and Discuss the Above Comments.

Let's Begin Tonight's Study

> **Acts 8:1–4 (NASB).** [1] Now **Saul approved of putting Stephen to death**. And on that day a great persecution began against the church in Jerusalem, and they all scattered throughout the regions of Judea and Samaria, except for the apostles. [2] Some devout men buried Stephen, and mourned loudly for him. [3] But **Saul began ravaging the church**, entering house after house; and he would drag away men and women and put them in prison. [4] Therefore, those who had been scattered went through places, preaching the word.

Commentary. We'll talk more about Saul next week. For now, let's just say Saul of Tarsus was leading the persecution against Christians.

As for Stephen, three important things happened because of his death:
1. Immediately, Saul began to persecute the Christians in Jerusalem.
2. Many believers left Jerusalem and traveled in different directions, spreading the good news of Jesus Christ *outside of Jerusalem.*
3. This resulted in the church growing throughout the region.

According to statistics from Open Doors (2020), more Christians are being persecuted for their faith today than any other time in history. History tells us that when believers are persecuted, the church experiences tremendous growth.

(Q) Are We on the Verge of the *Next Revival*? Why or Why Not?_____

(Q) Any Other Comments on These Verses?_____

Stop and Discuss the Above Verses and Questions. Answers to questions are on the next page.

Answers to Questions from the Previous Page

(Q) Are We on the Verge of the *Next Revival*? Why or Why Not?

Here are some statistics from Open Doors from 2020 (https://www.opendoorsusa.org/christian-persecution/):

- Over 260 million Christians living in places where they experience high levels of persecution
- 2,983 Christians killed for their faith
- 9,488 churches and other Christian buildings attacked
- 3,711 Christians detained without trial, arrested, sentenced, or imprisoned
- More Christians are being persecuted for their faith than any other time in history
- A Christian is killed for their faith every six minutes somewhere in the world
- Millions of believers live in places where they are oppressed, imprisoned, discriminated against, and even violently attacked—all because they believe in Jesus

Here are more statistics from Outside the Walls from 2020 (from https://www.rotw.com/):

- 92 percent of churchgoers say they do not plan to attend church more often after the COVID pandemic is over than they did before the pandemic began.
- 62 percent of all American churches are experiencing no growth and a decline in numbers.
- Americans' level of trust in religious leaders has sunk to 37 percent, the lowest Gallup has ever recorded.
- Only 12 percent of young people, ages 18–24, identify as Evangelical Christians.
- 70 percent of all young people who grow up in the church leave the church by their twenty's.
- More than 50 percent of young people (ages 18–24) do not believe the Bible is God's inspired word.
- Almost half of all Americans (44 percent) have no idea where they'll go when they die, but only 2 percent believe they'll go to hell.
- The majority of churchgoers (56 percent) say *they "pray for opportunities to share their faith,"* but in the last month, less than 10 percent had a conversation about the Lord with anyone.
- More than 2 million people per year have left the church for the past seven years.
- 51 percent of US churchgoers say they have never heard of the term *the Great Commission*.
- 25 percent of Evangelical Christians are not certain the physical resurrection of Jesus was a real event.

These statistics indicate that we may be losing the next generation! Let's Pray for A Revival.

> **Acts 8:5–8 (NASB).** ⁵ Philip went down to the city of Samaria and began proclaiming the Christ to them. ⁶ The crowds were paying attention with one mind to what was being said by Philip, as they heard and saw the signs [and wonders] which he was performing. ⁷ For in the case of many who had unclean spirits, they were coming out of them shouting with a loud voice; and many who had been paralyzed or limped on crutches were healed. ⁸ So there was much rejoicing in that city.

Commentary. Philip, like Stephen, was one of the seven men chosen to serve the people, making him a minister or deacon. **Do not confuse *this* Philip with the Apostle Philip.** This Philip was one of the 120 people who followed Jesus throughout his ministry. So we don't confuse the two Philips, let's call them *Philip the Deacon* and *Philip the Apostle*.

(Q) WHY WOULD IT BE DIFFICULT FOR PHILIP THE DEACON TO PREACH THE GOOD NEWS IN SAMARIA?

_____

(Q) ANY OTHER COMMENTS ON THESE VERSES?_____

STOP AND DISCUSS THE ABOVE VERSES AND QUESTIONS. Answers to questions are on the next page.

> **Acts 8:9–13 (NASB).** ⁹ Now a man named Simon had previously been practicing magic in the city and astonishing the people of Samaria, claiming to be someone great; ¹⁰ and all the people, from small to great, were paying attention to him, saying,
>   "*This man is the Power of God that is called Great.*"
> ¹¹ And they were paying attention to him because for a long time he had astounded them with his magic arts. ¹² But when they believed Philip as he was preaching the good news about the kingdom of God and the name of Jesus Christ, both men and women were being baptized. ¹³ Now even Simon himself believed; and after being baptized, he continued on with Philip, and as he observed signs and great miracles taking place, he was repeatedly amazed.

Commentary. Simon used magic so people would think he had God's power. But Simon's power did not come from God. One of Satan's biggest deceptions is to tempt people with the lie that they can "*be like God*" as he did to Eve in the Garden of Eden. Creating a false religion is Satan's main weapon against the Gospel. Today, there are plenty of false teachers, claiming to be Christians who are preaching about a new revelation from outside of the Bible.

(Q) HOW CAN WE RECOGNIZE FALSE TEACHERS?_____

(Q) ANY OTHER COMMENTS ON THESE VERSES?_____

STOP AND DISCUSS THE ABOVE VERSES AND QUESTIONS. Answers to questions are on the next page.

ANSWERS TO QUESTIONS FROM THE PREVIOUS PAGE

(Q) WHY WOULD IT BE DIFFICULT FOR PHILIP THE DEACON TO PREACH THE GOOD NEWS IN SAMARIA?

First reason—sorcerers and magic:

- In Samaria, there were many *sorcerers* and *magicians* who were *deceiving* the people.
- Some of these deceivers were claiming their power came from God.
- The Christian Samaritans were confused as to who was really preaching in the name of God.

Second reason—Jews did not like the Samaritans:

- The Samaritans intermarried with foreigners and were a mixed race.
- The Samaritans practiced a religion that was a combination of Judaism and idolatry.
- There was great hostility between the Jews and Samaritans.

(Q) HOW CAN WE RECOGNIZE *FALSE TEACHERS*?

- Christians should read and study the Bible so they can recognize false teachings.
- Christians should compare every teaching to the Bible.
- Christians should pray for discernment.

> **Acts 8:14–17 (NASB).** [14] Now when the apostles in Jerusalem heard that Samaria had received the word of God, they sent them Peter and John, [15] who came down and prayed for them that they would receive the Holy Spirit. [16] (For He had not yet fallen upon any of them; they had simply been baptized in the name of the Lord Jesus). [17] Then they began laying their hands on them, and they were receiving the Holy Spirit.

Commentary. As Christianity spread beyond Jerusalem into Samaria, word got back to the apostles that the Samaritans were becoming Christians. So the Jerusalem church sent Peter and John to investigate. What they found was that when the Samaritan believers were baptized, they did not receive the Holy Spirit. How come the Samaritan believers did not receive the Holy Spirit at the moment of salvation?

(Q) WHY DID GOD WAIT FOR PETER AND JOHN TO SEND THE HOLY SPIRIT TO THE SAMARITANS?

_____

(Q) ANY OTHER COMMENTS ON THESE VERSES?_____

> **STOP AND DISCUSS THE ABOVE VERSES AND QUESTIONS. Answers to questions are on the next page.**

> **Acts 8:18–24 (NASB).** [18] Now when Simon saw that the Spirit was given through the laying on of the apostles' hands, he offered them money, [19] saying,
> _"Give this authority to me as well, so that everyone on whom I lay my hands may receive the Holy Spirit."_
> [20] But Peter said to him,
> _"May your silver perish with you, because you thought you could acquire the gift of God with money! [21] You have no part or share in this matter, for your heart is not right before God. [22] Therefore, repent of this wickedness of yours, and pray to the Lord that, if possible, the intention of your heart will be forgiven you. [23] For I see that you are in the gall of bitterness and in the bondage of unrighteousness."_
> [24] But Simon answered and said,
> _"Pray to the Lord for me yourselves, so that nothing of what you have said may come upon me."_

Commentary. Simon the magician thought that Peter and John's power came from humans and that he could buy this power. Christians know the Holy Spirit is not for sale. Simon wanted to be a Christian for the wrong reasons and was _jealous_ of the apostles. _Simon's faith was not real._

Jealousy indicates that we are not satisfied with what God has given us. The Bible tells us to be content in all things. When we grumble and complain, it shows how worldly we _may_ still be.

REFLECTIVE QUESTION: _Am I content and grateful with God's blessings, or do I grumble and complain?_

(Q) WHAT WAS SIMON'S RESPONSE AFTER PETER REBUKED HIM?

_____

(Q) ANY OTHER COMMENTS ON THESE VERSES?_____

> **STOP AND DISCUSS THE ABOVE VERSES AND QUESTIONS. Answers to questions are on the next page.**

ANSWERS TO QUESTIONS FROM THE PREVIOUS PAGE

(Q) WHY DID GOD WAIT FOR PETER AND JOHN TO SEND THE HOLY SPIRIT TO THE SAMARITANS?

- The Bible does not say why the Samaritans did not receive the Holy Spirit immediately after their conversion. Only God knows the reason. Therefore, we are left to speculate.
- One reason might be that since the Jews and Samaritans hated one another, God was using Peter and John as eyewitnesses to testify the Holy Spirit came upon the Samaritan believers.
- Another reason could be that God was using Peter and John to unify the believers in Jerusalem with the believers in Samaria because it's quite possible that if the church in Samaria had started on its own, the Jews in Jerusalem may not have accepted them.

(Q) WHAT WAS SIMON'S RESPONSE AFTER PETER REBUKED HIM?

- Simon asked Peter to pray for him.
- He begged that nothing bad would happen to him.
- *The fear of the LORD is the beginning of wisdom. (Proverbs 9:10)*

Acts 8:25–29 (NASB). ²⁵ So, when [the apostles] had solemnly testified and spoken the word of the Lord, they started back to Jerusalem, and were preaching the gospel to many villages of the Samaritans. ²⁶ But **an angel of the Lord spoke to Philip**, **saying**,

"Get ready and go south to the road that descends from Jerusalem to Gaza" (This is a desert road). ²⁷ So Philip got ready and went; and there was an Ethiopian eunuch, a court official of Candace, queen of the Ethiopians, who was in charge of all her treasure; and he had come to Jerusalem to worship, ²⁸ and he was returning and sitting in his chariot, and was reading Isaiah the prophet. ²⁹ Then the Spirit said to Philip,

"Go up and join this chariot."

Commentary. The Ethiopian eunuch was probably a black man and a Jewish convert, who had traveled to Jerusalem to worship during Pentecost and was on his way home. According to Luke, the Ethiopian had a very important job and was in charge of the queen's treasures.

Philip was on his way back to Jerusalem when an angel told him to go south. Philip obeyed and changed his route, without knowing where he was going or why. You might call this a divine appointment between Philip and the Ethiopian eunuch.

OUR LESSON: As Christians, we must learn to listen for the Holy Spirit and obey. The Spirit will tell us where to go, what to do, and what to say. But first, we must be willing.

(Q) WHAT IS A EUNUCH?_____

(Q) ANY OTHER COMMENTS ON THESE VERSES?_____

STOP AND DISCUSS THE ABOVE VERSES AND QUESTIONS. Answers to questions are on the next page.

(Q) WHAT IS A EUNUCH?

- Natural eunuchs are born with one testicle.
- Unnatural eunuchs have been castrated voluntarily or involuntarily.
    - A voluntary eunuch is someone who has chosen to remain single and celibate in order to better serve the Lord.
    - An involuntary eunuch is someone who was forcibly castrated for some reason.

> **Acts 8:30–35 (NASB).** ³⁰ Philip ran up and heard him reading Isaiah the prophet, and said, *"Do you understand what you are reading?"* ³¹ And [the Ethiopian eunuch] said, *"Well, how could I, unless someone guides me?"*
>
> And he invited Philip to come up and sit with him. ³² Now the passage of Scripture which he was reading was this:
>
> > "HE WAS LED LIKE A SHEEP TO SLAUGHTER;   ← *Isaiah 53:7–8*
> > AND LIKE A LAMB THAT IS SILENT BEFORE ITS SHEARER,
> > SO HE DOES NOT OPEN HIS MOUTH.
> > ³³ IN HUMILIATION HIS JUSTICE WAS TAKEN AWAY;
> > WHO WILL DESCRIBE HIS GENERATION?
> > FOR HIS LIFE IS TAKEN AWAY FROM THE EARTH."
>
> ³⁴ The eunuch answered Philip and said,
> > *"Please tell me, of whom does the prophet say this? Of himself, or of someone else?"*
>
> ³⁵ Then Philip opened his mouth, and beginning from this Scripture he preached Jesus to him.

Commentary. The Ethiopian eunuch was reading Isaiah, but he did not understand the passage, so he asked Philip to explain it to him. The passage **foretold the crucifixion of Jesus**. Philip is a great example of a mature believer mentoring a new believer in Christ.

(Q) COMPARE THE FAITH OF THE ETHIOPIAN EUNUCH to SIMON THE MAGICIAN?_____

(Q) ANY OTHER COMMENTS ON THESE VERSES?_____

> STOP AND DISCUSS THE ABOVE VERSES AND QUESTIONS. **Answers to question are on the next page.**

> **Acts 8:36–40 (NASB).** ³⁶ As they went along the road they came to some water; and the eunuch said,
> > *"Look! Water!* **What prevents me from being baptized?"**
>
> ³⁸ And he ordered that the chariot stop; and they both went down into the water, Philip as well as the eunuch, and **he baptized him**. ³⁹ When they came up out of the water, the Spirit of the Lord snatched Philip away; and the eunuch no longer saw him, but went on his way rejoicing. ⁴⁰ But Philip found himself at Azotus, and as he passed through, he kept preaching the gospel to all the cities, until he came to Caesarea.

Commentary. Baptism is an important step that believers should take after deciding to follow Jesus. Water immersion represents the death of our old self, and coming out of the water represents being raised into new life in the same way Jesus rose from the dead.

> *REFLECTIVE QUESTION: As a Christian, have I been baptized? If not, why not?*

Notice that verse 37 is missing in the NASB translation but is in the KJV translation.
> And Philip said, *"If you believe with all your heart, you may [be baptized]."*
> And he answered and said, *"I believe that Jesus Christ is the Son of God." (Acts 8:37 KJV)*

(Q) WHY ARE THERE SO MANY BIBLE TRANSLATIONS?_____

(Q) ANY OTHER COMMENTS ON THESE VERSES?_____

> STOP AND DISCUSS THE ABOVE VERSES AND QUESTIONS. **Answers to question are on the next page.**

(Q) COMPARE THE FAITH OF THE ETHIOPIAN EUNUCH to SIMON THE MAGICIAN?

Simon the magician:

- He used magic so people would *think* he had God's power.
- His motive was to look important.
- His faith was not in Jesus but in himself.
- He was not a true believer.

Ethiopian eunuch:

- He had genuine faith.
- He had a desire to learn and study the scriptures.
- He had a desire to be baptized.
- He was humble.

(Q) WHY ARE THERE SO MANY BIBLE TRANSLATIONS?

- There are over fifty different English versions of the Bible.
- Some Bible versions **translate in a word for word**, literal method.
  - **Advantages**: It minimizes instances of the translator inserting their own interpretations into the passages.
  - **Disadvantages**: It can produce a translation so literal that it is not easily understood.
  - **Examples:** King James Version (KJV), New American Standard Bible (NASB).
- Some Bible versions **translate in a thought-for-thought** method.
  - **Advantages**: It usually produces a more readable and understandable Bible version.
  - **Disadvantages**: It has the potential for wrong interpretation.
  - **Examples**: The Living Bible (TLB), The Message (MSG).

Let's RE-Read Tonight's Verses

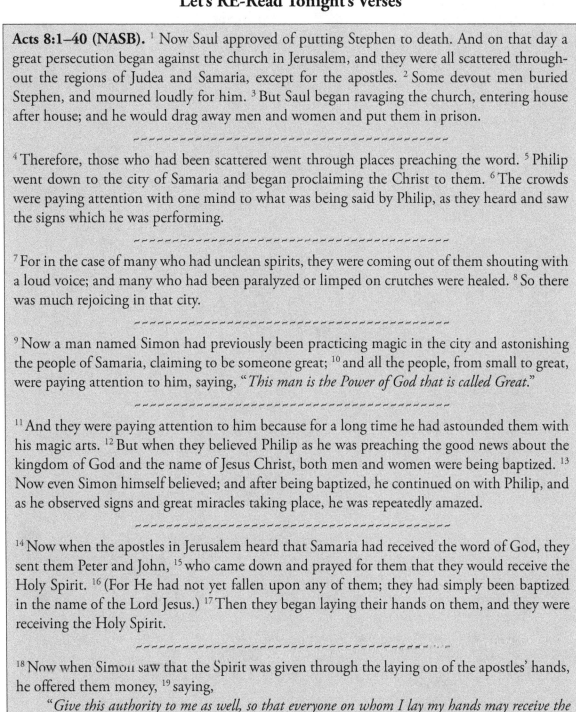

Acts 8:1–40 (NASB). ¹ Now Saul approved of putting Stephen to death. And on that day a great persecution began against the church in Jerusalem, and they were all scattered throughout the regions of Judea and Samaria, except for the apostles. ² Some devout men buried Stephen, and mourned loudly for him. ³ But Saul began ravaging the church, entering house after house; and he would drag away men and women and put them in prison.

⁴ Therefore, those who had been scattered went through places preaching the word. ⁵ Philip went down to the city of Samaria and began proclaiming the Christ to them. ⁶ The crowds were paying attention with one mind to what was being said by Philip, as they heard and saw the signs which he was performing.

⁷ For in the case of many who had unclean spirits, they were coming out of them shouting with a loud voice; and many who had been paralyzed or limped on crutches were healed. ⁸ So there was much rejoicing in that city.

⁹ Now a man named Simon had previously been practicing magic in the city and astonishing the people of Samaria, claiming to be someone great; ¹⁰ and all the people, from small to great, were paying attention to him, saying, *"This man is the Power of God that is called Great."*

¹¹ And they were paying attention to him because for a long time he had astounded them with his magic arts. ¹² But when they believed Philip as he was preaching the good news about the kingdom of God and the name of Jesus Christ, both men and women were being baptized. ¹³ Now even Simon himself believed; and after being baptized, he continued on with Philip, and as he observed signs and great miracles taking place, he was repeatedly amazed.

¹⁴ Now when the apostles in Jerusalem heard that Samaria had received the word of God, they sent them Peter and John, ¹⁵ who came down and prayed for them that they would receive the Holy Spirit. ¹⁶ (For He had not yet fallen upon any of them; they had simply been baptized in the name of the Lord Jesus.) ¹⁷ Then they began laying their hands on them, and they were receiving the Holy Spirit.

¹⁸ Now when Simon saw that the Spirit was given through the laying on of the apostles' hands, he offered them money, ¹⁹ saying,

> *"Give this authority to me as well, so that everyone on whom I lay my hands may receive the Holy Spirit."*

²⁰ But Peter said to him,

> *"May your silver perish with you, because you thought you could acquire the gift of God with money! ²¹ You have no part or share in this matter, for your heart is not right before God. ²² Therefore, repent of this wickedness of yours, and pray to the Lord that, if possible, the intention of your heart will be forgiven you. ²³ For I see that you are in the gall of bitterness and in the bondage of unrighteousness."*

²⁴ But Simon answered and said,

> *"Pray to the Lord for me yourselves, so that nothing of what you have said may come upon me."*

~~~~~~

²⁵ So, when they had solemnly testified and spoken the word of the Lord, they started back to Jerusalem, and were preaching the gospel to many villages of the Samaritans.

²⁶ But an angel of the Lord spoke to Philip, saying,

"Get ready and go south to the road that descends from Jerusalem to Gaza." (This is a desert road.)

~~~~~~

²⁷ So he got ready and went; and there was an Ethiopian eunuch, a court official of Candace, queen of the Ethiopians, who was in charge of all her treasure; and he had come to Jerusalem to worship, ²⁸ and he was returning and sitting in his chariot, and was reading Isaiah the prophet.

~~~~~~

²⁹ Then the Spirit said to Philip,

> *"Go up and join this chariot."*

³⁰ Philip ran up and heard him reading Isaiah the prophet, and said,

> *"Do you understand what you are reading?"*

³¹ And he said,

> *"Well, how could I, unless someone guides me?"*

And he invited Philip to come up and sit with him.

~~~~~~

³² Now the passage of Scripture which he was reading was this:

> *"HE WAS LED LIKE A SHEEP TO SLAUGHTER; AND LIKE A LAMB THAT IS SILENT BEFORE ITS SHEARER, SO HE DOES NOT OPEN HIS MOUTH.*
> *³³ IN HUMILIATION HIS JUSTICE WAS TAKEN AWAY;*
> *WHO WILL DESCRIBE HIS GENERATION?*
> *FOR HIS LIFE IS TAKEN AWAY FROM THE EARTH."*

³⁴ The eunuch answered Philip and said,

> *"Please tell me, of whom does the prophet say this? Of himself, or of someone else?"*

~~~~~~

³⁵ Then Philip opened his mouth, and beginning from this Scripture he preached Jesus to him.

³⁶ As they went along the road they came to some water; and the eunuch said,

> *"Look! Water! What prevents me from being baptized?"*

³⁸ And he ordered that the chariot stop; and they both went down into the water, Philip as well as the eunuch, and he baptized him.

~~~~~~

> [39] When they came up out of the water, the Spirit of the Lord snatched Philip away; and the eunuch no longer saw him, but went on his way rejoicing. [40] But Philip found himself at Azotus, and as he passed through he kept preaching the gospel to all the cities, until he came to Caesarea.

(Q) ANY FINAL COMMENTS?_____

THIS IS THE END OF THIS WEEK'S STUDY.

A Precept Bible Study

ACTS

The Birth of the Church

Week 9, Acts 9:1–43

A Verse-by-Verse Journey through the book of Acts

Notes

Let's Review Last Week's Study

Stephen's death began a great persecution against **the Way** led by Saul of Tarsus. The persecution resulted in Philip the Deacon and many other believers fleeing Jerusalem and spreading the word of God throughout the outer regions of Judea and Samaria.

Word got back to the elders in Jerusalem, so they sent Peter and John to Samaria to investigate. When they got to Samaria, a magician named Simon tried to buy the power of the Holy Spirit, so Peter rebuked him because his motives for following Jesus were wrong.

When Philip left Samaria, an angel of the Lord told him to head south. Philip obeyed and ran into an Ethiopian eunuch who was reading Isaiah. Philip told the eunuch that he was reading about a prophecy foretelling the crucifixion of Jesus. When Philip finished explaining the passage, he baptized the eunuch.

(Q) ANY OTHER COMMENTS ON CHAPTER 8?_____

STOP AND DISCUSS THE ABOVE COMMENTS.

Let's Begin Tonight's Study

> **Acts 9:1–2 (NASB).** [1] Now **Saul**, still breathing threats and murder against the disciples of the Lord, went to the high priest, [2] and asked for letters from him to the synagogues in Damascus, so that if he found any belonging to **the Way**, whether men or women, he might bring them in shackles to Jerusalem.

Commentary. Saul wanted to track down the believers who ran away and bring them to Jerusalem for persecution. In order to do this, he needed a *letter of approval* from the *high priest*.

(Q) IN VERSE 2, WHY WERE BELIEVERS CALLED "*THE WAY*"?_____

(Q) ANY OTHER COMMENTS ON THESE VERSES?_____

STOP AND DISCUSS THE ABOVE VERSES AND QUESTIONS. Answers to questions are on the next page.

> **Acts 9:3–6 (NASB).** [3] Now as [Saul] was traveling, it happened that he was approaching Damascus, and suddenly a light from heaven flashed around him; [4] and he fell to the ground and heard a voice saying to him, "*Saul, Saul, why are you persecuting Me?*"
> [5] And he said, "*Who are You, Lord?*"
> And He said, "*I am Jesus whom you are persecuting,* [6] *get up and enter the city, and it will be told to you what you must do.*"

(Q) SAUL KNEW THE VOICE WAS FROM THE LORD, SO WHY WOULD HE BE SURPRISED WHEN JESUS RESPONDED, "*I am Jesus whom you are persecuting*"?_____

(Q) ANY OTHER COMMENTS ON THESE VERSES?_____

STOP AND DISCUSS THE ABOVE VERSES AND QUESTIONS. Answers to questions are on the next page.

(Q) IN VERSE 2, WHY WERE BELIEVERS CALLED "*THE WAY*"?

- The early followers of Christ referred to themselves as **followers of the Way** because Jesus said, "*I am the way and the truth and the life*" (John 14:6).

(Q) SAUL KNEW THE VOICE WAS FROM THE LORD, SO WHY WOULD HE BE SURPRISED WHEN JESUS RESPONDED, "*I am Jesus whom you are persecuting*"?

- Saul believed he was doing God's work by killing followers of Jesus.
- Now he found out that Jesus Is the Messiah.
- Saul might have had a hard time wrapping his head around this news that he was killing God's people instead of doing God's work.

> **Acts 9:7–17 (NASB).** [7] The men who traveled with him stood speechless, hearing the voice but seeing no one. [8] Saul got up from the ground, and though his eyes were open, he could see nothing; and leading him by the hand, they brought him into Damascus. [9] And for three days he was without sight, and neither ate nor drank. [10] Now there was a disciple in Damascus named Ananias; and the Lord said to him in a vision,
>
> *"Ananias."*
>
> And he said,
>
> *"Here I am, Lord."*
>
> [11] And the Lord said to him,
>
> *"Get up and go to the street called Straight, and inquire at the house of Judas for a man from Tarsus named Saul, for he is praying, [12] and he has seen in a vision a man named Ananias come in and lay his hands on him, so that he might regain his sight."*
>
> [13] But Ananias answered,
>
> *"Lord, I have heard from many people about this man, how much harm he did to Your saints in Jerusalem; [14] and here he has authority from the chief priests to arrest all who call on Your name."*
>
> [15] But the Lord said to him,
>
> *"Go, for **he is a chosen instrument of Mine**, to bear My name before the Gentiles and kings and the sons of Israel; [16] **for I will show him how much he must suffer in behalf of My name**."*
>
> [17] So Ananias departed and entered the house, and after laying his hands on him said,
>
> *"Brother Saul, the Lord Jesus, who appeared to you on the road by which you were coming, has sent me so that you may regain your sight and be filled with the Holy Spirit."*

Commentary. This was Paul's road to Damascus experience where Jesus told him that he was chosen by God to preach to the Gentiles.

What about Ananias? Verse 10 called him a disciple, which meant he was a follower of the Way. In Acts 22, Luke described him as *a faithful man with a good reputation among the people*. We also know from these verses that Ananias was obedient and very brave for going into a dangerous situation to pray with a known murderer named Saul. Ananias was a loving and compassionate man because he greeted Saul as a brother.

OUR LESSON: It is not easy to show love to someone that we may be afraid of or doubt their motives; therefore, we need the power of the Holy Spirit to have godly love.

(Q) IN VERSE 15, WHAT DOES IT MEAN "*he is a chosen instrument of Mine*"?

_____

(Q) IN verse 15, WHAT DOES IT MEAN "*I will show him how much he must suffer in behalf of My name*"?

_____

(Q) ANY OTHER COMMENTS ON THESE VERSES?_____

STOP AND DISCUSS THE ABOVE VERSES AND QUESTIONS. Answers to questions are on the next page.

(Q) IN VERSE 15, WHAT DOES IT MEAN "*he is a chosen instrument of Mine*"?

- Jesus chose Saul to be His mouthpiece to the Gentiles.
- Jesus chose Saul to show that He can use anyone for His purposes.
- Saul was set apart from birth and called by God's grace to "*preach among the Gentiles.*"

But when God set me apart even from my mother's womb and called me through His grace was pleased to reveal His Son in me so that I might preach Him among the Gentiles. (Galatians 1:15–16)

(Q) IN VERSE 15, WHAT DOES IT MEAN "*I will show him how much he must suffer in behalf of My name*"?

- We know that Paul suffered much for his faith because he wrote about this in his second letter to the Corinthians.

Five times I received from the Jews thirty-nine lashes. Three times I was beaten with rods, once I was stoned, three times I was shipwrecked, a night and a day I have spent adrift at sea. I have been on frequent journeys, in dangers from rivers, dangers from robbers, dangers from my countrymen, dangers from the Gentiles, dangers in the city, dangers in the wilderness, dangers at sea, dangers among false brothers; I have been in labor and hardship, through many sleepless nights, in hunger and thirst, often without food, in cold and exposure. (2 Corinthians 11:24–27)

- **How does this affect me?** Everyone who follows Jesus must be willing to suffer. Jesus warned us that people will persecute and hate believers.

If the world hates you, keep in mind that it hated me first. If you belonged to the world, it would love you as its own. As it is, you do not belong to the world, but I have chosen you out of the world. That is why the world hates you. Remember what I told you: "A servant is not greater than his master." If they persecuted me, they will persecute you also. (John 15:18–20)

> **Acts 9:18–22 (NASB).** [18] And immediately something like **fish scales fell from his eyes**, and he regained his sight, and he got up and was baptized; [19] and he took food and was strengthened. Now for several days he was with the disciples who were in Damascus, [20] and immediately he began to proclaim Jesus in the synagogues, saying, *"He is the Son of God."*
> [21] All those hearing him continued to be amazed, and were saying,
>> *"Is this not the one who in Jerusalem destroyed those who called on this name, and had come here for the purpose of bringing them bound before the chief priests?"*
> [22] But Saul kept increasing in strength and confounding Jews who lived in Damascus by proving that this Jesus is the Christ.

Commentary. It is understandable that the Jews and Christians were confused and skeptical about Saul. *Yesterday* he was killing Christians, and *today* he is worshipping Jesus and wants to be friends.

It was probably that way with you. When the scales covering your heart fell off, you were able to see that Jesus is the Son of God, and your family and friends may not understand the change in you. It takes a while to build trust after being reborn in the spirit.

(Q) BRIEFLY DESCRIBE YOUR CONVERSION MOMENT._____

(Q) ANY OTHER COMMENTS ON THESE VERSES?_____

STOP AND DISCUSS THE ABOVE VERSES AND QUESTIONS. Answers to questions are on the next page.

> **Acts 9:23–26 (NASB).** [23] When **many days had elapsed**, the Jews plotted together to do away with him, [24] but their plot became known to Saul. They were also closely watching the gates day and night so that they might put him to death; [25] but his disciples took him at night and let him down through an opening in the wall, lowering him in a large basket. [26] **When he came to Jerusalem, he tried repeatedly to associate with the disciples; and yet they were all afraid of him, as they did not believe that he was a disciple.**

Commentary. *"Many days"* referred to the three years Paul spent in Arabia after his conversion.

- (30 AD) Jesus was baptized and began His ministry.
- (33 AD) The crucifixion/resurrection and the birth of the Church.
- (34 AD) Paul's conversion. Then he went to Arabia for three years.
- (37 AD) Paul returned to Jerusalem and tried to meet with the Apostles.

When Paul heard some unbelieving Jews were plotting to kill him, his disciples helped him escape and go to Jerusalem. However, the apostles were afraid of Paul and did not believe he was a disciple.
I bet it was that way with you too; your old reputation was hard to shake after you became a Christian.

(Q) WHEN YOU BECAME A CHRISTIAN, WHAT OBSTACLES DID YOU FACE?_____

(Q) ANY OTHER COMMENTS ON THESE VERSES?_____

STOP AND DISCUSS THE ABOVE VERSES AND QUESTIONS. Answers to questions are on the next page.

Answers to Questions from the Previous Page

(Q) Briefly Describe Your Conversion Moment.

- Testimony time. Limit each person to about two minutes.

(Q) When You Became a Christian, What Obstacles Did You Face?

- People did not believe I had really changed or that it would last.
- People did not want to be around me because I talked about Jesus.
- People tempted me to go back to my old life.
- Ask if anyone else wants to share about the obstacles they faced.

> **Acts 9:27–28 (NASB).** ²⁷ But **Barnabas took hold of him and brought him to the apostles** and described to them how he had seen the Lord on the road, and that He had talked to him, and how Paul had spoken out boldly in the name of Jesus at Damascus. ²⁸ And he was with them, moving about freely in Jerusalem, speaking out boldly in the name of the Lord.

Commentary. Luke did not tell us *how* Barnabas knew Paul, but he did tell us that Barnabas believed in Paul's conversion and introduced him to the apostles. We know from Paul's letter to the Galatians that he only met with two apostles in Jerusalem.

> *I went away to Arabia, and returned once more to Damascus. Then three years later I went up to Jerusalem to become acquainted with Cephas, and stayed with him for fifteen days. But I did not see another one of the apostles except James, the Lord's brother.* (Galatians 1:17–19)

(Q) WHAT DO WE KNOW ABOUT BARNABAS?_____

(Q) ANY OTHER COMMENTS ON THESE VERSES?_____

STOP AND DISCUSS THE ABOVE VERSES AND QUESTIONS. Answers to questions are on the next page.

> **Acts 9:29–31 (NASB).** ²⁹ And [Paul] was talking and arguing with the Hellenistic Jews; but they were attempting to put him to death. ³⁰ Now when the brothers learned of it, they brought him down to Caesarea and sent him away to Tarsus.
> ³¹ **So the church throughout Judea, Galilee, and Samaria enjoyed peace**, as it was being built up; and as it continued in the fear of the Lord and in the comfort of the Holy Spirit, it kept increasing.

Commentary. The Hellenistic Jews did not live in Jerusalem and did not speak Hebrew. They were from other countries and regions outside of Judea. They did not like Paul preaching about Jesus, so they plotted to kill Him. When some Christians heard about the plot, they tried to protect Paul and sent him to his hometown of Tarsus for his own safety. We know from Paul's letter to the Galatians that he continued to preach in Samaria and Cilicia for about seven years before Barnabas came to get him to go to Antioch and disciple the new Gentile believers.

(Q) WHAT DOES *"continued in the fear of the Lord"* MEAN?_____

(Q) IN verse 31, WHY WOULD THE CHURCHES *"enjoyed peace"* DURING THIS TIME?

_____

(Q) ANY OTHER COMMENTS ON THESE VERSES?_____

STOP AND DISCUSS THE ABOVE VERSES AND QUESTIONS. Answers to questions are on the next page.

(Q) WHAT DO WE KNOW ABOUT BARNABAS?

- He was a *"good man, full of the Holy Spirit and faith"* (Acts 11:24).
- His name means *"Son of Encouragement"* (Acts 4:36).
- Barnabas brought Paul to the apostles when they did not believe he was a follower of Christ (Acts 9:27).
- He accompanied Paul on his first missionary trip and helped plant many churches throughout Galatia (Acts 13).
- Barnabas and Paul spent a year in Antioch and started the first Gentile church in Antioch (Acts 11:25–30).
- His cousin was John Mark, who wrote the Gospel of Mark and accompanied Barnabas on Paul's first missionary journey. John Mark did **not** complete the journey and abruptly left Paul and Barnabas.
- After Paul and Barnabas completed their missionary journey, Barnabas wanted to take John Mark on the next journey. This caused a rift between Paul and Barnabas, and they parted ways (Acts 15:36–41).
- Barnabas spent time discipling John Mark and took him on his next journey. Paul replaced Barnabas with Silas and took him on his second journey.

(Q) WHAT DOES *"continued in the fear of the Lord"* MEAN?

- A love for God and a desire to please Him.
- A reverence for God and a desire to worship Him.

(Q) IN VERSE 31, WHY WOULD THE CHURCHES *"enjoyed peace"* DURING THIS TIME?

- The biggest reason for peace in the region was because the man formerly known as **Saul of Tarsus was no longer persecuting Christians**.
- Paul leaving the region and going to Asia for three years helped to quiet the conflict against Christians and allowed Paul to prove his commitment to his newfound faith in Jesus.
- After three years in Asia, Paul returned to Jerusalem and met with Peter and James, but he ran into some trouble with the Hellenistic Jews who tried to kill him.
- Paul was escorted out of town and went back home to Tarsus where he spent the next seven to eight years preaching the good news throughout Syria and Cilicia.

> **Acts 9:32–35 (NASB).** ³² Now as Peter was traveling through all those regions, he also came down to the saints who lived at Lydda. ³³ There he found a man named Aeneas who had been bedridden for eight years, because he was paralyzed. ³⁴ Peter said to him,
> *"Aeneas, Jesus Christ heals you; get up and make your own bed."*
> Immediately he got up. ³⁵ And all who lived at Lydda and Sharon saw him, and they turned to the Lord.

Commentary. Now that peace had come to the region, believers in **the Way** were no longer in danger, so Peter was able to leave Jerusalem and preach in cities outside of Judea. Peter traveled to Lydda to visit the saints, and while he was there, he healed a crippled man.

(Q) WHY DOES PETER REFER TO BELIEVERS AS SAINTS?_____

(Q) ANY OTHER COMMENTS ON THESE VERSES?_____

STOP AND DISCUSS THE ABOVE VERSES AND QUESTIONS. Answers to questions are on the next page.

> **Acts 9:36–43 (NASB).** ³⁶ Now in Joppa there was a disciple named Tabitha (which when translated means Dorcas); this woman was excelling in acts of kindness and charity which she did habitually. ³⁷ But it happened at that time that she became sick and died; and when they had washed her body, they laid it in an upstairs room. ³⁸ Since Lydda was near Joppa, the disciples, having heard that Peter was there, sent two men to him, urging him, *"Do not delay in coming to us."*
> ³⁹ So Peter got ready and went with them. When he arrived, they brought him into the room upstairs; and all the widows stood beside him, weeping and showing all the tunics and garments that Dorcas used to make while she was with them. ⁴⁰ But Peter sent them all out and knelt down and prayed, and turning to the body, he said, *"**Tabitha, arise.**"*
> And she opened her eyes, and when she saw Peter, she sat up. ⁴¹ And he gave her his hand and raised her up; and calling the saints and widows, he presented her alive. ⁴² It became known all over Joppa, and many believed in the Lord. ⁴³ And Peter stayed in Joppa many days with a tanner named Simon.

Commentary. Word about the miracle in Lydda spread, and when a Christian woman named Tabitha died in Joppa, two disciples went to Lydda to ask Peter to come and help. How do we know Tabitha was a Christian? We know this because Luke called her a disciple. Tabitha lived out her faith through her good works of kindness and charity. When Peter got to Lydda, he performed another miracle and brought Tabitha back to life!

(Q) WHY DID THE WIDOWS SHOW PETER *"the tunics and garments"* THAT TABITHA MADE?

_____

(Q) WHAT IS THE DIFFERENCE BETWEEN DOING GOOD WORKS OUT OF OBLIGATION AND DOING GOOD WORKS HABITUALLY?_____

(Q) ANY OTHER COMMENTS ON THESE VERSES?_____

STOP AND DISCUSS THE ABOVE VERSES AND QUESTIONS. Answers to questions are on the next page.

(Q) WHY DOES PETER REFER TO BELIEVERS AS SAINTS?

- The word **saint** comes from the Greek word **hagios**, which means **set apart for the Lord** and is used sixty-eight times in the Bible.
- In other words, **saint refers to anyone who is a follower of Jesus**.
- If you grew up Catholic, this may come as a surprise to you because you were taught sainthood was only for special people. According to the Bible, ALL followers of Christ are called saints. This is because when Jesus went to the cross, He took on the sins of the world so that when a believer stands before God on judgment day, He will see a perfect and righteous child of God and not their sin.

(Q) WHY DID THE WIDOWS SHOW PETER *"the tunics and garments"* THAT TABITHA MADE?

- They probably wanted Peter to know that **Tabitha was a generous Christian woman** who gave to the widows and the poor, and they were grateful for her kindness.

(Q) WHAT IS THE DIFFERENCE BETWEEN DOING GOOD WORKS OUT OF OBLIGATION AND DOING GOOD WORKS HABITUALLY?

- Habitually means giving regularly rather than once in a while.
- Therefore, giving habitually implies giving sacrificially because the giving is done regardless of circumstances.
- On the other hand, a person who gives out of obligation or only when they have a few extra dollars in their pocket, *may* need to check their motives.
- The Bible says giving or not giving is a heart condition:

Each one must do just as he has purposed in his heart, not grudgingly or under compulsion, for God loves a cheerful give. (2 Corinthians 9:7)

Honor the Lord from your wealth, And from the first of all your produce; So your barns will be filled with plenty, And your vats will overflow with new wine. (Proverbs 3:9–10)

There is one who scatters [gives], and yet increases all the more, And there is one who withholds what is justly due, and yet it results only in want. (Proverbs 11:24)

Let's RE-Read Tonight's Verses

Acts 9:1–43 (NASB). [1] Now Saul, still breathing threats and murder against the disciples of the Lord, went to the high priest, [2] and asked for letters from him to the synagogues in Damascus, so that if he found any belonging to the Way, whether men or women, he might bring them in shackles to Jerusalem.

- -

[3] Now as he was traveling, it happened that he was approaching Damascus, and suddenly a light from heaven flashed around him; [4] and he fell to the ground and heard a voice saying to him,

> *"Saul, Saul, why are you persecuting Me?"*

[5] And he said,

> *"Who are You, Lord?"*

And He said,

> *"I am Jesus whom you are persecuting, [6] but get up and enter the city, and it will be told to you what you must do."*

- -

[7] The men who traveled with him stood speechless, hearing the voice but seeing no one. [8] Saul got up from the ground, and though his eyes were open, he could see nothing; and leading him by the hand, they brought him into Damascus. [9] And for three days he was without sight, and neither ate nor drank.

- -

[10] Now there was a disciple in Damascus named Ananias; and the Lord said to him in a vision,

> *"Ananias."*

And he said, *"Here I am, Lord."*

[11] And the Lord said to him,

> *"Get up and go to the street called Straight, and inquire at the house of Judas for a man from Tarsus named Saul, for he is praying, [12] and he has seen in a vision a man named Ananias come in and lay his hands on him, so that he might regain his sight."*

- -

[13] But Ananias answered,

> *"Lord, I have heard from many people about this man, how much harm he did to Your saints in Jerusalem; [14] and here he has authority from the chief priests to arrest all who call on Your name."*

[15] But the Lord said to him,

> *"Go, for he is a chosen instrument of Mine, to bear My name before the Gentiles and kings and the sons of Israel; [16] for I will show him how much he must suffer in behalf of My name."*

- -

[17] So Ananias departed and entered the house, and after laying his hands on him said,

> *"Brother Saul, the Lord Jesus, who appeared to you on the road by which you were coming, has sent me so that you may regain your sight and be filled with the Holy Spirit."*

- -

¹⁸ And immediately something like fish scales fell from his eyes, and he regained his sight, and he got up and was baptized; ¹⁹ and he took food and was strengthened. Now for several days he was with the disciples who were in Damascus, ²⁰ and immediately he began to proclaim Jesus in the synagogues, saying,

> *"He is the Son of God."*

~~~~~~

²¹ All those hearing him continued to be amazed, and were saying,

> *"Is this not the one who in Jerusalem destroyed those who called on this name, and had come here for the purpose of bringing them bound before the chief priests?"*

²² But Saul kept increasing in strength and confounding Jews who lived in Damascus by proving that this Jesus is the Christ.

~~~~~~

²³ When many days had elapsed, the Jews plotted together to do away with him, ²⁴ but their plot became known to Saul. They were also closely watching the gates day and night so that they might put him to death; ²⁵ but his disciples took him at night and let him down through an opening in the wall, lowering him in a large basket.

~~~~~~

²⁶ When he came to Jerusalem, he tried repeatedly to associate with the disciples; and yet they were all afraid of him, as they did not believe that he was a disciple. ²⁷ But Barnabas took hold of him and brought him to the apostles and described to them how he had seen the Lord on the road, and that He had talked to him, and how he had spoken out boldly in the name of Jesus at Damascus.

~~~~~~

²⁸ And he was with them, moving about freely in Jerusalem, speaking out boldly in the name of the Lord. ²⁹ And he was talking and arguing with the Hellenistic Jews; but they were attempting to put him to death. ³⁰ Now when the brothers learned of it, they brought him down to Caesarea and sent him away to Tarsus. ³¹ So the church throughout Judea, Galilee, and Samaria enjoyed peace, as it was being built up; and as it continued in the fear of the Lord and in the comfort of the Holy Spirit, it kept increasing.

~~~~~~

³² Now as Peter was traveling through all those regions, he also came down to the saints who lived at Lydda. ³³ There he found a man named Aeneas who had been bedridden for eight years, because he was paralyzed. ³⁴ Peter said to him,

> *"Aeneas, Jesus Christ heals you; get up and make your own bed."*

Immediately he got up. ³⁵ And all who lived at Lydda and Sharon saw him, and they turned to the Lord.

~~~~~~

³⁶ Now in Joppa there was a disciple named Tabitha (which when translated means Dorcas); this woman was excelling in acts of kindness and charity which she did habitually. ³⁷ But it happened at that time that she became sick and died; and when they had washed her body, they laid it in an upstairs room.

- -

³⁸ Since Lydda was near Joppa, the disciples, having heard that Peter was there, sent two men to him, urging him,

"*Do not delay in coming to us.*"

³⁹ So Peter got ready and went with them. When he arrived, they brought him into the room upstairs; and all the widows stood beside him, weeping and showing all the tunics and garments that Dorcas used to make while she was with them.

- -

⁴⁰ But Peter sent them all out and knelt down and prayed, and turning to the body, he said,

"*Tabitha, arise.*"

And she opened her eyes, and when she saw Peter, she sat up. ⁴¹ And he gave her his hand and raised her up; and calling the saints and widows, he presented her alive. ⁴² It became known all over Joppa, and many believed in the Lord. ⁴³ And Peter stayed in Joppa many days with a tanner named Simon.

(Q) ANY FINAL COMMENTS?_____

THIS IS THE END OF THIS WEEK'S STUDY.

A Precept Bible Study

ACTS

The Birth of the Church

Week 10, Acts 10:1–48

A Verse-by-Verse Journey through the book of Acts

Let's Review Last Week's Study

- After Stephen's death, persecution against the Christians intensified and was led by Saul of Tarsus.
- Then Saul had a conversion experience on the road to Damascus and became a believer.
- Jesus told Paul he would be His *"mouthpiece to the Gentiles."*
- The apostles and disciples doubted Paul's conversion and refused to meet with him. Barnabas stepped in and took Paul to meet with Peter and James.
- The church experienced a season of peace after Saul, the biggest persecutor, was no longer a threat.
- Now that it was safe to leave Jerusalem, Peter traveled to Lydda, and through the power of the Holy Spirit, he healed a paralyzed man.
- Next Peter traveled to Joppa and performed another miracle when he brought back to life a woman named Tabitha.

(Q) WHAT ELSE DO YOU REMEMBER ABOUT CHAPTER 9?_____

STOP AND DISCUSS THE ABOVE COMMENTS.

Let's Begin Tonight's Study

Acts 10:1–2 (NASB). [1] Now there was a man in Caesarea named **Cornelius, a centurion** of what was called the Italian cohort, [2] a devout man and one who feared God with all his household, and made many charitable contributions to the Jewish people and prayed to God continually.

Commentary. In these verses, we meet a Gentile believer named Cornelius. He was a Roman Officer in the military and was a generous man who loved God and was a man of prayer.

One other tidbit worth mentioning is that throughout Luke's Letter, he referred to the Gentile believers as those who *"Feared God"* or were *"God-Fearers."* When Luke used these terms, he was referring to a Gentile believer.

- A Gentile who became a Christian was called a "God-Fearer."
- A Gentile who converted to Judaism and then became a Christian was called a "God-Fearing Proselyte."

Cornelius was a Gentile Christian who had not been circumcised; therefore, he was a "God-Fearer."

(Q) FROM THESE VERSES, WHAT ELSE DO WE KNOW ABOUT CORNELIUS?_____

(Q) WHAT IS THE DIFFERENCE BETWEEN BEING GOD-FEARING and BEING FEARFUL OF GOD?

_____

(Q) ANY OTHER COMMENTS ON THESE VERSES?_____

STOP AND DISCUSS THE ABOVE VERSES AND QUESTIONS. **Answers to questions are on the next page.**

(Q) From These Verses, What Else Do We Know about Cornelius?

- He was a *captain* in the Italian army, also known as a *centurion*.
- He was a *Gentile* and a Roman citizen.
- He was a *follower of Jesus*.
- His entire family were *followers of Jesus*.
- He was a *generous* man.
- He was a man of *prayer*.

(Q) What Is the Difference between Being God-Fearing and Being Fearful Of God?

- For the **unbeliever**, the fear of God is the fear of the judgment of God and eternal death. Therefore, **the unbeliever is fearful of God**.
  - Death is eternal separation from God.
  - Death is eternal darkness.
  - Death is eternal torment.
- For the **believer**, the fear of God is much different. **The believer's fear is reverence for God**.
  - Reverence is a desire to please God, like a child wants to please their parents.
  - Reverence is taking sin seriously.
  - The fear of the LORD is the beginning of knowledge (Proverbs 1:7).
  - The fear of LORD is respecting Him, obeying Him, submitting to Him, and worshiping Him.

> **Acts 10:3–8 (NASB).** ³ **About the ninth hour of the day he clearly saw in a vision an angel of God** who had just come in and said to him, "*Cornelius!*"
> ⁴ And he looked at him intently and became terrified, and said,
> "*What is it, lord?*"
> And [**the angel**] **said to him**,
> "*Your prayers and charitable gifts have ascended as a memorial offering before God.* ⁵ *Now dispatch some men to Joppa and send for a man named Simon, who is also called Peter;* ⁶ *he is staying with a tanner named Simon, whose house is by the sea.*"
> ⁷ When the angel who spoke to him left, he summoned two of his servants and a devout soldier from his personal attendants, ⁸ and after he had explained everything to them, he sent them to Joppa.

Commentary. These verses show that Cornelius was obedient because even though he was "*terrified of the angel,*" he immediately sent two servants and a soldier to Joppa to get Peter. The angel might have been Gabriel who God used many times to deliver messages to His people. Notice that one of the soldiers was a "*devout soldier,*" which meant that he was a believer.

Cornelius probably did not know who Peter was nor that he had just performed two miracles and was undoubtedly in high demand. A huge obstacle facing Cornelius was the Jews looked down on Gentiles and it was unheard of for a Gentile like Cornelius to ask a Jew into his home, especially a Jew of Peter's status.

(Q) If Gabriel Is a Messenger for God, What Angel Is a Warrior for God?

_____

(Q) Any Other Comments on These Verses?_____

STOP AND DISCUSS THE ABOVE VERSES AND QUESTIONS. Answers to questions are on the next page.

> **Acts 10:9–12 (NASB).** ⁹ On the next day, as they were on their way and approaching the city, Peter went up on the housetop about the sixth hour to pray. ¹⁰ But he became hungry and wanted to eat; but while they were making preparations, **he fell into a trance**; ¹¹ and he saw the sky opened up, and an object like a great sheet coming down, lowered by four corners to the ground, ¹² and on it were all kinds of four-footed animals and crawling creatures of the earth and birds of the sky.

Commentary. Another name for trance is dream, which meant that Peter fell asleep and was dreaming about unclean animals (we'll discuss the meaning of his dream in the next verses). God used dreams many times in the Bible to communicate with people.

(Q) What Other Times in the Bible Did God Use Dreams to Communicate with People?

_____

(Q) Any Other Comments on These Verses?_____

STOP AND DISCUSS THE ABOVE VERSES AND QUESTIONS. Answers to questions are on the next page.

Answers to Questions from the Previous Page

(Q) If Gabriel Is a Messenger for God, What Angel Is a Warrior for God?

- Michael the Archangel is a warrior in God's army (Jude 1:9, 1 Thessalonians 4:16, Revelation 12:7).
- Angels have other functions such as ministering to believers (Hebrews 1:14) and worshiping and praising God (Psalm 148:2).
- Another function angels provide is delivering messages from God to believers (Luke 1:19, Luke 1:26, Daniel 8:16).
- The term guardian angel is never mentioned in Scripture; however, the concept is commonly assumed (Genesis 21:17–20, 1 Kings 19:5–7, Matthew 18:10, Luke 1:11–20).

(Q) What Other Times in the Bible Did God Use Dreams to Communicate with People?

- We know that Joseph, the son of Jacob, had many prophetic dreams (Genesis 37:1–11).
- God also used dreams in *nonbelievers*, such as when Pharaoh asked Joseph to interpret his dreams. Another example is when Pontius Pilate's wife had a dream warning Pilate to let Jesus go.

Here are a few verses where God used dreams and visions:

- *After these things the word of the Lord came to Abram **in a vision**, saying, "Do not fear, Abram, I am a shield to you; your reward shall be very great"* (Genesis 15:1).
- *In Gibeon the Lord appeared to Solomon **in a dream** at night; and God said, "Ask what you wish Me to give you"* (1 Kings 3:5).
- *But when he had thought this over, behold, an angel of the Lord appeared to him **in a dream**, saying, "Joseph, son of David, do not be afraid to take Mary as your wife; for the Child who has been conceived in her is of the Holy Spirit"* (Matthew 1:20).

> **Acts 10:11–16 (NASB).** [11] He saw the sky opened up, and an object like a great sheet coming down, lowered by four corners to the ground, [12] and on it were all kinds of four-footed animals and crawling creatures of the earth and birds of the sky.
> [13] A voice came to him, *"Get up, Peter, kill and eat!"*
> [14] But Peter said, *"By no means, Lord, for I have never eaten anything unholy and unclean."*
> [15] Again a voice came to him a second time, ***"What God has cleansed, no longer consider unholy."***
> [16] This happened three times, and immediately the object was taken up into the sky.

Commentary. Here is where the story gets interesting. Cornelius, a Gentile, just sent several men to get Peter, and at the same time, Peter was having this crazy dream about eating *unclean animals*. God was using Peter's dream to show him that Christians were not bound by the *kosher law in Leviticus* and that no one should be considered unclean, which meant that salvation is open to all who repent and follow Jesus, *even Gentiles*.

(Q) WHAT WAS THE CONNECTION BETWEEN PETER'S DREAM AND CORNELIUS SENDING FOR HIM?

_____

(Q) ANY OTHER COMMENTS ON THESE VERSES?_____

STOP AND DISCUSS THE ABOVE VERSES AND QUESTIONS. Answers to questions are on the next page.

> **Acts 10:17–18 (NASB).** [17] Now while Peter was greatly perplexed in mind as to what the vision which he had seen might mean, behold, the men who had been sent by Cornelius had asked directions to Simon's house, and they appeared at the gate; [18] and calling out, they were asking whether Simon, who was also called Peter, was staying there.

Commentary. God's timing is perfect! While Peter was perplexed and trying to understand his dream, the men sent by Cornelius showed up at his door. In the next verses, the Holy Spirit clears up Peter's confusion.

(Q) WHEN YOU GET *"PERPLEXED"* LIKE PETER WAS, WHAT CAN YOU DO TO MAKE A GODLY DECISION?

_____

(Q) ANY OTHER COMMENTS ON THESE VERSES?_____

STOP AND DISCUSS THE ABOVE VERSES AND QUESTIONS. Answers to questions are on the next page.

Answers to Questions from the Previous Page

(Q) What Was the Connection between Peter's Dream and Cornelius Sending for Him?

- God used Peter's dream to prepare his heart to accept an invitation from Cornelius, a Gentile.
- God used an angel and a dream to simultaneously prepare Cornelius and Peter for this divine meeting.

(Q) When You Get "*Perplexed*" Like Peter Was, What Can You Do to Make a Godly Decision?

- Pray and meditate.
- Read your Bible.
- Seek counsel from a mature Christian.
- Evaluate your options: Will this go against God's Word or lead to sin?
- The more we **listen** for God's voice, the better we get at recognizing His voice and distinguishing it from the noise of the world.

> **Acts 10:19–23a (NASB).** ¹⁹ While Peter was reflecting on the vision, **the Spirit said to him**, *"Behold, three men are looking for you. ²⁰ But get up, go downstairs and accompany them without misgivings, for I have sent them Myself."* ²¹ Peter went down to the men and said, *"Behold, I am the one you are looking for; what is the reason for which you have come?"* ²² They said, *"Cornelius, a centurion, a righteous and God-fearing man, well-spoken of by the entire nation of the Jews, was divinely directed by a holy angel to send for you to come to his house and hear a message from you."* ²³ So [Peter] invited them in and gave them lodging.

Commentary. The men were waiting outside because Gentiles were not allowed in a Jewish home. An angel prepared Peter for this meeting and the Holy Spirit told Peter that these men were sent by God Himself! Consequently, Peter invited them to stay with him. Prior to his dream, Peter would have never invited a Gentile into his home.

(Q) Any Other Comments on These Verses?_____

Stop and Discuss the Above Comments

> **Acts 10:23b–29 (NASB).** Now on the next day, Peter got ready and went away with them, and some of the brothers from Joppa accompanied him. ²⁴ On the following day he entered Caesarea. Now Cornelius was expecting them and had called together his relatives and close friends. ²⁵ When Peter entered, Cornelius met him, and fell at his feet and worshiped him. ²⁶ But Peter helped him up, saying, *"Stand up; I, too, am just a man."* ²⁷ As he talked with him, he entered and found many people assembled. ²⁸ And [Peter] **said to them**, *"You yourselves know that it is forbidden for a Jewish man to associate with or visit a foreigner; and yet **God has shown me that I am not to call any person unholy or unclean**. ²⁹ That is why I came without even raising any objection when I was sent for."*

Commentary. Can you imagine the excitement Cornelius had, *anticipating the arrival of Peter the Apostle?* When Cornelius saw Peter, he bowed down to worship him. However, Peter immediately told Cornelius to get up. **By his actions, Peter was saying, "We are equals."** Then in verse 28, Peter told Cornelius's household that God told him that the Jews should no longer consider the Gentiles as *unclean*. In other words, the Jewish Christians and Gentile Christians were equals.

(Q) When You Became a Christian, What Old Ideas about God Changed?

_____

(Q) Any Other Comments On These Verses?_____

Stop and Discuss the Above Verses and Questions. Answers to questions are on the next page.

Answers to Questions from the Previous Page

(Q) When You Became a Christian, What Old Ideas about God Changed?

- Testimony time.
- Each person (that wants to) should give a short testimony of old ideas that they struggled with letting go of after they became a Christian.

> **Acts 10:29b–33 (NASB).** [Peter asked Cornelius] *"So I ask, for what reason did you send for me?"* ³⁰ Cornelius said,
>
>> *"Four days ago, to this hour, I was praying in my house during the ninth hour; and behold, a man stood before me in shining clothing,* ³¹ *and he said,*
>>
>>> *'Cornelius, your prayer has been heard and your charitable gifts have been remembered before God.* ³² *Therefore send some men to Joppa and invite Simon, who is also called Peter, to come to you; he is staying at the house of Simon the tanner, by the sea.'*
>>
>> ³³ *So I sent men to you immediately, and you have been kind enough to come. Now then, we are all here present before God to hear everything that you have been commanded by the Lord."*

Commentary. Cornelius told Peter an angel of light (in shining clothes) told him his prayers had been answered and to call for Peter to bring them a message from God. Obviously, Cornelius's household were "on fire for the Lord" and were eager to hear from Peter.

OUR LESSON: May I have the same eagerness as Cornelius's household each time I hear a word from God.

(Q) DESCRIBE A TIME WHEN GOD ANSWERED A PRAYER THROUGH A DIVINE APPOINTMENT OR SITUATION THAT WAS UNDENIABLY FROM GOD._____

(Q) ANY OTHER COMMENTS ON THESE VERSES?_____

STOP AND DISCUSS THE ABOVE VERSES AND QUESTIONS. Answers to question are on the next page.

(Q) Describe a Time When God Answered a Prayer through a Divine Appointment or Situation That Was Undeniably from God.

- Testimony time.
- Each person (that wants to), give a short testimony of a time when God answered a prayer by arranging a situation that seemed like a coincidence but in hindsight was orchestrated by God.

> **Acts 10:34-48 (NASB).** 34 Opening his mouth, **Peter said:**
>
> *"I most certainly understand now that God is not one to show partiality,* 35 *but in every nation the one who fears Him and does what is right is acceptable to Him.* 36 *The word which He sent to the sons of Israel, preaching peace through Jesus Christ (He is Lord of all)—* 37 *you yourselves know the thing that happened throughout Judea, starting from Galilee, after the baptism which John proclaimed.*
>
> 38 *You know of Jesus of Nazareth, how God anointed Him with the Holy Spirit, and with power, and how He went about doing good and healing all who were oppressed by the devil, for God was with Him.* 39 *We are witnesses of all the things that He did both in the country of the Jews and in Jerusalem.*
>
> *They also put Him to death by hanging Him on a cross.* 40 *God raised Him up on the third day and granted that He be revealed,* 41 *not to all the people, but to witnesses who had been chosen beforehand by God, that is, to us who ate and drank with Him after He arose from the dead.* 42 *And He ordered us to preach to the people, and to testify solemnly that this is the One who has been appointed by God as Judge of the living and the dead.* 43 *All the prophets testify of Him, that through His name everyone who believes in Him receives forgiveness of sins."*
>
> 44 **While Peter was still speaking these words, the Holy Spirit fell upon all those who were listening to the message.** 45 All the Jewish believers who came with Peter were amazed, because the gift of the Holy Spirit had also been poured out on the Gentiles. 46 For they were hearing [the Gentiles] speaking with tongues and exalting God. Then Peter responded,
>
> 47 *"Surely no one can refuse the water for these to be baptized, who have received the Holy Spirit just as we did, can he?"*
>
> 48 And he ordered them to be baptized in the name of Jesus Christ. Then they asked him to stay on for a few days.

Commentary. Peter described Jesus's life from the time He was baptized with the Holy Spirit to His death and ascension into heaven. **While Peter was still preaching, the Holy Spirit came upon all who were there, including the Gentiles.** This was a defining moment in the early church, proving to the Jewish believers that God accepted the Gentiles and that anyone who repented and called on the name of Jesus would receive the forgiveness of their sins.

Notice the Holy Spirit came upon the believers before they were baptized. Earlier in Acts, the Holy Spirit came upon the believers after they were baptized. It just goes to show that baptism is not a condition of salvation. However, believers are encouraged to be baptised as a public acknowledgment of their faith.

(Q) WHAT OTHER TIME DID THE HOLY SPIRIT COME AND BELIEVERS STARTED TALKING IN TONGUES?

_____

(Q) WHO WERE THE WITNESSES IN **verses 40–41?**_____

(Q) ANY OTHER COMMENTS ON THESE VERSES?_____

STOP AND DISCUSS THE ABOVE VERSES AND QUESTIONS. Answers to questions are on the next page.

Answers to Questions from the Previous Page

(Q) What Other Time Did the Holy Spirit Come and Believers Started Talking in Tongues?

- The same thing happened during **Pentecost** when Peter was preaching and three thousand Jewish men gave their lives to Jesus (Acts, chapter 2).
- This is commonly referred to as the Birth of the Church.

(Q) Who Were the Witnesses in Verses 40–41?

- The *witnesses* were the twelve apostles, the women and the 120 family and friends who followed Jesus for three and a half years.
- After Jesus rose from the dead, there was a total of five hundred people who saw Jesus alive.

Let's RE-Read Tonight's Verses

Acts 10:1–48 (NASB). [1] Now there was a man in Caesarea named Cornelius, a centurion of what was called the Italian cohort, [2] a devout man and one who feared God with all his household, and made many charitable contributions to the Jewish people and prayed to God continually.

- -

[3] About the ninth hour of the day he clearly saw in a vision an angel of God who had just come in and said to him, *"Cornelius!"*
[4] And he looked at him intently and became terrified, and said, *"What is it, lord?"*

- -

And he said to him,
> *"Your prayers and charitable gifts have ascended as a memorial offering before God. [5] Now dispatch some men to Joppa and send for a man named Simon, who is also called Peter; [6] he is staying with a tanner named Simon, whose house is by the sea."*

- -

[7] When the angel who spoke to him left, he summoned two of his servants and a devout soldier from his personal attendants, [8] and after he had explained everything to them, he sent them to Joppa. [9] On the next day, as they were on their way and approaching the city, Peter went up on the housetop about the sixth hour to pray.

- -

[10] But he became hungry and wanted to eat; but while they were making preparations, he fell into a trance; [11] and he saw the sky opened up, and an object like a great sheet coming down, lowered by four corners to the ground, [12] and on it were all kinds of four-footed animals and crawling creatures of the earth and birds of the sky. [13] A voice came to him,
> *"Get up, Peter, kill and eat!"*

- -

[14] But Peter said,
> *"By no means, Lord, for I have never eaten anything unholy and unclean."*
[15] Again a voice came to him a second time,
> *"What God has cleansed, no longer consider unholy."*
[16] This happened three times, and immediately the object was taken up into the sky.

- -

[17] Now while Peter was greatly perplexed in mind as to what the vision which he had seen might mean, behold, the men who had been sent by Cornelius had asked directions to Simon's house, and they appeared at the gate; [18] and calling out, they were asking whether Simon, who was also called Peter, was staying there.

- -

[19] While Peter was reflecting on the vision, the Spirit said to him,
> *"Behold, three men are looking for you. [20] But get up, go downstairs and accompany them without misgivings, for I have sent them Myself."*
[21] Peter went down to the men and said,
> *"Behold, I am the one you are looking for; what is the reason for which you have come?"*

- -

²² They said,

"Cornelius, a centurion, a righteous and God-fearing man well spoken of by the entire nation of the Jews, was divinely directed by a holy angel to send for you to come to his house and hear a message from you."

²³ So he invited them in and gave them lodging.

- -

Now on the next day he got ready and went away with them, and some of the brothers from Joppa accompanied him. ²⁴ On the following day he entered Caesarea. Now Cornelius was expecting them and had called together his relatives and close friends. ²⁵ When Peter entered, Cornelius met him, and fell at his feet and worshiped him.

- -

²⁶ But Peter helped him up, saying,

"Stand up; I, too, am just a man."

²⁷ As he talked with him, he entered and found many people assembled. ²⁸ And he said to them,

"You yourselves know that it is forbidden for a Jewish man to associate with or visit a foreigner; and yet God has shown me that I am not to call any person unholy or unclean. ²⁹ That is why I came without even raising any objection when I was sent for. So I ask, for what reason did you send for me?"

- -

³⁰ Cornelius said,

"Four days ago to this hour, I was praying in my house during the ninth hour; and behold, a man stood before me in shining clothing, ³¹ and he said,
'Cornelius, your prayer has been heard and your charitable gifts have been remembered before God. ³² Therefore send some men to Joppa and invite Simon, who is also called Peter, to come to you; he is staying at the house of Simon the tanner, by the sea.'"

- -

³³ *"So I sent men to you immediately, and you have been kind enough to come. Now then, we are all here present before God to hear everything that you have been commanded by the Lord."*

- -

³⁴ Opening his mouth, Peter said:

"I most certainly understand now that God is not one to show partiality, ³⁵ but in every nation the one who fears Him and does what is right is acceptable to Him."

- -

³⁶ *"The word which He sent to the sons of Israel, preaching peace through Jesus Christ (He is Lord of all)—³⁷ you yourselves know the thing that happened throughout Judea, starting from Galilee, after the baptism which John proclaimed. ³⁸ You know of Jesus of Nazareth, how God anointed Him with the Holy Spirit and with power, and how He went about doing good and healing all who were oppressed by the devil, for God was with Him.*

- -

39 We are witnesses of all the things that He did both in the country of the Jews and in Jerusalem. They also put Him to death by hanging Him on a cross. 40 God raised Him up on the third day and granted that He be revealed, 41 not to all the people, but to witnesses who had been chosen beforehand by God, that is, to us who ate and drank with Him after He arose from the dead."

- -

42 "And He ordered us to preach to the people, and to testify solemnly that this is the One who has been appointed by God as Judge of the living and the dead. 43 All the prophets testify of Him, that through His name everyone who believes in Him receives forgiveness of sins."

- -

44 While Peter was still speaking these words, the Holy Spirit fell upon all those who were listening to the message. 45 All the Jewish believers who came with Peter were amazed, because the gift of the Holy Spirit had also been poured out on the Gentiles. 46 For they were hearing them speaking with tongues and exalting God.

- -

Then Peter responded,
47 "Surely no one can refuse the water for these to be baptized, who have received the Holy Spirit just as we did, can he?"

48 And he ordered them to be baptized in the name of Jesus Christ. Then they asked him to stay on for a few days.

(Q) ANY FINAL COMMENTS?_____

THIS IS THE END OF THIS WEEK'S STUDY.

A Precept Bible Study

ACTS

The Birth of the Church

Week 11, Acts 11:1–30

A Verse-by-Verse Journey through the book of Acts

Let's Review Last Week's Study

- Last week we met a Gentile believer named Cornelius who was a captain in the Italian cohort (military). He was a generous man and a man of prayer, and he had a good reputation among all the Jewish nations.
- An angel spoke to Cornelius and told him that his prayers had been heard by God and that he should send some men to get Peter the Apostle and bring him to his home.
- Simultaneously, Peter was having a dream about unclean animals and the Lord spoke to him and said, "***What God has cleansed, no longer consider unholy.***"
- While Peter was pondering this dream, the men sent by Cornelius arrived at Peter's house.
- Then the Lord spoke to Peter again and said, "*I have sent them, go with them without misgivings.*"
- Peter realized his dream and the voice of the Lord were telling him that the dietary restrictions in Leviticus ended *when Jesus died on the cross* and fulfilled the Old Testament law.
- This meant that no one, including Gentiles, should be considered unclean.
- Peter went with the men to Cornelius's house and gave a sermon on Jesus.
- While he was talking, the Holy Spirit came upon all who were listening, including the Gentiles.
- **This was a defining moment in the early church, proving to the Jewish believers that God accepted Gentiles** and that ANYONE who repented and called on the name of Jesus would be saved!

(Q) What Else Do You Remember about Chapter 10?_____

STOP AND DISCUSS THE ABOVE COMMENTS

Let's Begin Tonight's Study

> **Acts 11:1–3 (NASB).** [1] Now the apostles and the brothers and sisters who were throughout Judea heard that the Gentiles also had received the word of God. [2] **And when Peter came up to Jerusalem, the Jewish believers took issue with him**, [3] saying, *"You went to uncircumcised men and ate with them."*

Commentary. Up until now, salvation had been limited to the Jews living in and around Judea. This chapter signified a change where the Gospel began spreading throughout the Mediterranean and salvation came to everyone, including the Gentiles.

(Q) Why Would Jewish Believers "*Take Issue*" with Peter for "*Preaching*" to the Gentiles?

_____

(Q) Any Other Comments on These Verses?_____

STOP AND DISCUSS THE ABOVE VERSES AND QUESTIONS. **Answers to questions are on the next page.**

Answers to Questions from the Previous Page

(Q) Why Would Jewish Believers *"Take Issue"* with Peter for *"Preaching"* to the Gentiles?

- The Jewish believers were not upset that Peter preached to the Gentiles. They were upset that he ate a meal with the Gentiles in their home.
- The Jews had been taught their whole lives that it was unlawful for a Jew to eat with a Gentile because they were unclean. Even Peter thought this before he went to see Cornelius.

  Peter said to them, "You yourselves know that it is forbidden for a Jewish man to associate with or visit a foreigner; and yet God has shown me that I am not to call any person unholy or unclean." (Acts 10:28)

- Can you imagine how difficult it must have been for the Jews to let go of a life time of being taught that certain animals and people were unclean, and now they find out that's not true?
- Not only that, but they also find out that the Jewish ceremonies and traditions they held near and dear to their heart were no longer required for a relationship with God or needed for salvation.
- It's easy to see why some Jewish believers *"took issue with Paul"* for going to see the Gentiles.

> **Acts 11:4–12 (NASB).** ⁴ But **Peter began and explained at length to them in an orderly sequence**, saying,
>
> ⁵ *"I was in the city of Joppa praying; and in a trance I saw a vision, an object coming down like a great sheet lowered by four corners from the sky; and it came to where I was,* ⁶ *and I stared at it and was thinking about it, and I saw the four-footed animals of the earth, the wild animals, the crawling creatures, and the birds of the sky.* ⁷ *I also heard a voice saying to me,*
>
> *'Get up, Peter; kill and eat.'*
>
> ⁸ *But I said, 'By no means, Lord, for nothing unholy or unclean has ever entered my mouth.'*
>
> ⁹ *But a voice from heaven answered a second time,*
>
> **'What God has cleansed, no longer consider unholy.'**
>
> ¹⁰ *This happened three times, and everything was drawn back up into the sky.* ¹¹ *And behold, at that moment three men who had been sent to me from Caesarea came up to the house where we were staying.* ¹² *And* **the Spirit told me to go with them without misgiving***s. These six brothers also went with me, and we entered the man's house."*

Commentary. Peter began by telling the Jews God told him three times that nothing was to be considered unclean and that he should go to the Cornelius's house without hesitation. In the previous chapter, Peter said, *"You yourselves know that it is forbidden for a Jewish man to associate with or visit a foreigner; and yet God has shown me that I am not to call any person unholy or unclean"* (Acts 10:28).

(Q) Cornelius Only Asked for Peter. Why Would Peter Take Six Men with Him?

_____

(Q) Any Other Comments on These Verses?_____

> **Stop and Discuss the Above Verses and Questions. Answers to questions are on the next page.**

> **Acts 11:13–18 (NASB).** ¹³ *"And [Cornelius] reported to us how he had seen the angel standing in his house, and saying,*
>
> *'Send some men to Joppa and have Simon, who is also called Peter, brought here;* ¹⁴ *and he will speak words to you by which you will be saved, you and all your household.'*
>
> ¹⁵ *And as I began to speak,* **the Holy Spirit fell upon them just as He did upon us at the beginning***.* ¹⁶ *And I remembered the word of the Lord, how He used to say,*
>
> *'John baptized with water, but you will be baptized with the Holy Spirit.'*
>
> ¹⁷ **Therefore, if God gave them the same gift as He also gave to us after believing in the Lord Jesus Christ, who was I that I could stand in God's way?"**
>
> ¹⁸ When they heard this, they quieted down and glorified God, saying,
>
> *"Well then, God has also granted to the Gentiles the repentance that leads to life."*

Commentary. As Peter was telling his story, he reminded the Jewish believers that Jesus told them they would be baptized with the Holy Spirit, and who were they to decide who gets the Spirit and who doesn't!

(Q) What Was the Purpose of Peter Retelling His Story?_____

(Q) Any Other Comments on These Verses?_____

> **Stop and Discuss the Above Verses and Questions. Answers to questions are on the next page.**

Answers to Questions from the Previous Page

(Q) Cornelius Only Asked for Peter. Why Would Peter Take Six Men with Him?

- To help carry supplies.
- For protection.
- To be witnesses.

(Q) What Was the Purpose of Peter Retelling His Story?

- The Jewish believers were angry with Peter for going into a Gentile's home and he needed to "*quiet them down,*" so he told them that it was **God who commanded him to go see Cornelius and give a message of salvation**.
- It was God who told him three times that no animal or person should be considered unclean, including the Gentiles.
- And finally, it was God who sent the Holy Spirit to come upon the Gentiles just like the Holy Spirit came upon the Jews during Pentecost.
- In other words, it was always part of God's plan for salvation to come to the Gentiles.

> **Acts 11:19–21 (NASB).** [19] So then those who were scattered because of the persecution that occurred in connection with Stephen made their way to Phoenicia, Cyprus, and Antioch, speaking the word to no one except to Jews alone. [20] **But there were some of them, men of Cyprus and Cyrene, who came to Antioch and began speaking to the Greeks as well, preaching the good news of the Lord Jesus.** [21] And the hand of the Lord was with them, and a large number who believed turned to the Lord.

Commentary. Most Jewish believers from Jerusalem only shared the good news with other Jews, making Christianity *seem like a sect of Judaism.* It wasn't until some Jewish believers went to Antioch and shared the good news with the Greeks that people began looking at Christianity as its own religion. This was also the beginning of the Gospel spreading beyond Judea into Syria and Cilicia.

(Q) IN VERSE 19, WHO WERE "*those who scattered*"?_____

(Q) ANY OTHER COMMENTS ON THESE VERSES?_____

STOP AND DISCUSS THE ABOVE VERSES AND QUESTIONS. Answers to questions are on the next page.

> **Acts 11:22–24 (NASB).** [22] **The news about them reached the ears of the church in Jerusalem, and they sent Barnabas off to Antioch.** [23] Then when he arrived and witnessed the grace of God, he rejoiced and began to encourage them all with resolute heart to remain true to the Lord; [24] for he was a good man, and full of the Holy Spirit and faith. And considerable numbers were added to the Lord.

Commentary. So far, we have seen the church grow because of four different events:

1. During Pentecost, Peter preached to three thousand Jews, and the Holy Spirit came upon them. This was the birth of the church.
2. Then Peter preached to another five thousand, *and many more turned to the Lord.*
3. Then Peter preached at Cornelius's house. And the Holy Spirit came upon the Gentiles, *and many turned to the Lord.*
4. Then the believers who were being persecuted in Jerusalem scattered and began spreading the good news to the Greeks in Antioch and throughout Syria and Cilicia, *and many more turned to the Lord.*

These last two events caught the attention of the church in Jerusalem, **so the elders sent Barnabas to Antioch to see what was happening.** We previously met Barnabas in Acts, chapter 4, when he "*sold a tract of land*" and "*gave the money*" to the apostles to distribute among the poor.

(Q) WHAT DO YOU REMEMBER ABOUT BARNABAS?_____

(Q) ANY OTHER COMMENTS ON THESE VERSES?_____

STOP AND DISCUSS THE ABOVE VERSES AND QUESTIONS. Answers to questions are on the next page.

Answers to Questions from the Previous Page

(Q) IN VERSE 19, WHO WERE *"those who scattered"*?

- These were Jewish believers who were in Jerusalem for Pentecost who fled to safety in neighbouring cities to get away from the persecution after Stephen was stoned to death.

  Those who were scattered because of the persecution that occurred in connection with Stephen made their way to Phoenicia, Cyprus, and Antioch. (Acts 11:19)

(Q) WHAT DO YOU REMEMBER ABOUT BARNABAS?

- He was a *"good man, full of the Holy Spirit and faith"* (Acts 11:24).
- He was a generous man (Acts 4).
- He was an encourager (Acts 4:36).
- Barnabas brought Paul to the apostles when they did not believe he was a follower of Christ (Acts 9:27).
- He accompanied Paul on his first missionary trip to Galatia (Acts 13).
- Barnabas and the Apostle Paul started the first Gentile church in Antioch (Acts 11:25–30).
- John Mark and Barnabas were cousins (John Mark wrote the Gospel of Mark).
- Barnabas mentored John Mark and took him on a missionary journey.

> **Acts 11:25–26a (NASB).** ²⁵ And [Barnabas] left for Tarsus to look for Saul; ²⁶ and when he had found him, he brought him to Antioch. And for an entire year they met with the church and taught considerable numbers of people.

Commentary. Antioch was an important trade center consisting of Jews and Greeks. Barnabas was a Hellenistic Jew who spoke Greek and was the perfect choice to go to Antioch.

As for Saul, after his conversion to the Apostle Paul, he went to Asia for three years before returning to Jerusalem and meeting with Peter and James. After their meeting, Paul went to Syria and Cilicia to preach the good news. This was the beginning of Paul's ministry.

By the time Barnabas went to get Paul, he had been preaching in Syria and Cilicia for about 7–8 years (Galatians 1:21–24).

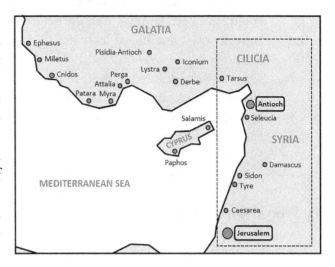

(Q) WHY DID BARNABAS SELECT SAUL TO GO WITH HIM TO ANTIOCH?_____

(Q) ANY OTHER COMMENTS ON THESE VERSES?_____

REFLECTIVE QUESTION: Do I actively look for opportunities to mentor new believers? For example, am I leading or participating in a small group in my church? When was the last time I shared the Gospel with a family member, or friend or neighbor?

STOP AND DISCUSS THE ABOVE VERSES AND QUESTIONS. Answers to questions are on the next page.

> **Acts 11:26b (NASB).** ²⁶ And the **disciples were first called Christians in Antioch.**

Commentary. Today, most believers would say that the term *Christian* means *"Christlike"* or *"follower of Christ."* However, in the early church, there was another meaning for Christian.

(Q) WHO WERE THE FIRST PEOPLE TO USE THE TERM CHRISTIAN AND WHY?_____

(Q) ANY OTHER COMMENTS ON THESE VERSES?_____

STOP AND DISCUSS THE ABOVE VERSES AND QUESTIONS. Answer to questions are on the next page.

Answers to Questions from the Previous Page

(Q) Why Did Barnabas Select Saul to Go with Him to Antioch?

- The Apostle Paul had already been preaching in Syria and Cilicia for seven to eight years and would have been familiar with the believers in Antioch.
- Antioch was a mixture of Jews and Gentiles and Paul was called to preach to the Gentiles (Acts 9:15).
- Paul was well educated in the Torah and would be able to gain the respect of the Jews and he was a Roman citizen and would be able to gain the respect of the Gentiles too.
- Antioch was a new church with new believers who needed to be discipled and Barnabas needed help mentoring so many new converts.

(Q) Who Were the First People to Use the Term Christian and Why?

- The early church called themselves **The Way** and did not call themselves Christians.
- Only nonbelievers called them Christians.
- The **pagans** in Antioch were clever with words and made up the word *Christian* to make fun of the believers. In other words, the term Christian was originally used as a joke. This changed after Peter used the term in Antioch.

> **Acts 11:27–30 (NASB).** 27 Now at this time some prophets came down from Jerusalem to Antioch. 28 One of them, named Agabus, stood up and indicated by the Spirit that there would definitely be a severe famine all over the world. And this took place in the reign of Claudius. 29 And to the extent that any of the disciples had means, each of them determined to send a contribution for the relief of the brothers and sisters living in Judea. 30 And they did this, sending it with Barnabas and Saul to the elders.

Commentary. Claudius was the emperor from AD 41 to AD 54. During this period, there were five famines in the Roman Empire. As a result of **Agabus's prophecy**, the Gentile believers in Antioch sent money to the Jewish believers in Judea in preparation for the famine (v. 29–30).

The money sent from the church at Antioch demonstrated unity between the Gentile believers and the Jewish believers in the church in Jerusalem. By sending money, the believers continued the practice of **Christian socialism** described in Acts 4, where believers voluntarily gave money and goods to the apostles, who then distributed the goods to the poor, based on need.

(Q) WHAT IS A PROPHET?_____

(Q) WHAT IS THE DIFFERENCE BETWEEN CHRISTIAN SOCIALISM AND POLITICAL SOCIALISM?

_____

(Q) ANY OTHER COMMENTS ON THESE VERSES?_____

STOP AND DISCUSS THE ABOVE VERSES AND QUESTIONS. Answers to questions are on the next page.

(Q) WHAT IS A PROPHET?

- A prophet is someone chosen by God to speak for God.
- The purpose of a prophet is to deliver messages from God, as 2 Peter 1:21 says.

For no prophecy was ever made by an act of human will, but men moved by the Holy Spirit spoke from God. (2 Peter 1:21)

- A prophet should be tested to know if they are from God, as 1 John 4:1–2 says.

Beloved, do not believe every spirit, but test the spirits to see whether they are from God, because many false prophets have gone out into the world. By this you know the Spirit of God. (1 John 4:1–2)

(Q) WHAT IS THE DIFFERENCE BETWEEN CHRISTIAN SOCIALISM AND POLITICAL SOCIALISM?

Political socialism:

- An economic and political system in which property, natural resources, and the means of production are owned and **managed by the government** rather than by individuals or private companies.
- In this system, wealth is **involuntarily** taken from the rich and redistributed to the poor so that the wealth is spread out equally.

Christian socialism in the early church:

- People **voluntarily** shared their money and possessions with the church.
- The **church** manages and distributes goods, not the government.
- There are **no** Bible verses that call for a mandate to redistribute wealth; however, God does command us to give to the church and give to the less fortunate.

Each one must do just as he has decided in his heart, not reluctantly or under compulsion, for God loves a cheerful giver. (2 Corinthians 9:7)

Let's RE-Read Tonight's Verses

Acts 11:1–30 (NASB). [1] Now the apostles and the brothers and sisters who were throughout Judea heard that the Gentiles also had received the word of God. [2] And when Peter came up to Jerusalem, the Jewish believers took issue with him, [3] saying,

"You went to uncircumcised men and ate with them."

- -

[4] But Peter began and explained at length to them in an orderly sequence, saying,

[5] *"I was in the city of Joppa praying; and in a trance I saw a vision, an object coming down like a great sheet lowered by four corners from the sky; and it came to where I was, [6] and I stared at it and was thinking about it, and I saw the four-footed animals of the earth, the wild animals, the crawling creatures, and the birds of the sky."*

- -

[7] *"I also heard a voice saying to me,*
'Get up, Peter; kill and eat.'
[8] *But I said,*
'By no means, Lord, for nothing unholy or unclean has ever entered my mouth.'
[9] *But a voice from heaven answered a second time,*
'What God has cleansed, no longer consider unholy.'"

- -

[10] *"This happened three times, and everything was drawn back up into the sky. [11] And behold, at that moment three men who had been sent to me from Caesarea came up to the house where we were staying. [12] And the Spirit told me to go with them without misgivings."*

- -

"These six brothers also went with me, and we entered the man's house. [13] And he reported to us how he had seen the angel standing in his house, and saying,
'Send some men to Joppa and have Simon, who is also called Peter, brought here; [14] and he will speak words to you by which you will be saved, you and all your household.'"

- -

[15] *"And as I began to speak, the Holy Spirit fell upon them just as He did upon us at the beginning. [16] And I remembered the word of the Lord, how He used to say,*
'John baptized with water, but you will be baptized with the Holy Spirit.'
[17] *Therefore, if God gave them the same gift as He also gave to us after believing in the Lord Jesus Christ, who was I that I could stand in God's way?"*

- -

[18] When they heard this, they quieted down and glorified God, saying,

"Well then, God has also granted to the Gentiles the repentance that leads to life."

[19] So then those who were scattered because of the persecution that occurred in connection with Stephen made their way to Phoenicia, Cyprus, and Antioch, speaking the word to no one except to Jews alone.

- -

²⁰ But there were some of them, men of Cyprus and Cyrene, who came to Antioch and began speaking to the Greeks as well, preaching the good news of the Lord Jesus. ²¹ And the hand of the Lord was with them, and a large number who believed turned to the Lord. ²² The news about them reached the ears of the church in Jerusalem, and they sent Barnabas off to Antioch.

²³ Then when he arrived and witnessed the grace of God, he rejoiced and began to encourage them all with resolute heart to remain true to the Lord; ²⁴ for he was a good man, and full of the Holy Spirit and faith. And considerable numbers were added to the Lord.

²⁵ And he left for Tarsus to look for Saul; ²⁶ and when he had found him, he brought him to Antioch. And for an entire year they met with the church and taught considerable numbers of people; and the disciples were first called Christians in Antioch.

²⁷ Now at this time some prophets came down from Jerusalem to Antioch. ²⁸ One of them, named Agabus, stood up and indicated by the Spirit that there would definitely be a severe famine all over the world. And this took place in the reign of Claudius.

²⁹ And to the extent that any of the disciples had means, each of them determined to send a contribution for the relief of the brothers and sisters living in Judea. ³⁰ And they did this, sending it with Barnabas and Saul to the elders.

(Q) ANY FINAL COMMENTS?_____

THIS IS THE END OF THIS WEEK'S STUDY.

A Precept Bible Study

ACTS

The Birth of the Church

Week 12, Acts 12:1–25

A Verse-by-Verse Journey through the book of Acts

Notes

Let's Review Last Week's Study

- Last week, the Jewish believers in Judea were angry with Peter because he went to Cornelius's house.
- In order to *"quiet down"* the Jews, Peter told them that an angel commanded him to go see Cornelius and give a message from God, and while he was preaching, the Holy Spirit came upon the Gentiles.
- After the Jewish believers heard this, they accepted the Gentiles into the faith.
- At the same time, the believers who left Judea because of persecution were preaching throughout Syria and Cilicia, resulting in many Gentiles coming to the Lord, especially in the city of Antioch.
- The disciples heard what was happening in Antioch and sent Barnabas to investigate.
- Barnabas took Saul with him, and when they saw what was happening, they stayed in Antioch for a year to teach and encourage the new Gentile believers.
- Antioch became the first Gentile church and was very important as Christianity spread beyond Judea.
- The pagans in Antioch made fun of the believers and mocked them by calling them Christ-*ians*. This was the first the time the term *Christian* was used to describe followers of the Way.
- A prophet named Agabus told the disciples that a famine was coming.
- When the Gentile believers in Antioch heard about the prophecy, they sent money to the church in Jerusalem in preparation for the famine, thus uniting the two churches.

(Q) WHAT ELSE DO YOU REMEMBER ABOUT CHAPTER 11?_____

STOP AND DISCUSS THE ABOVE COMMENTARY.

Let's Begin Tonight's Study

> **Acts 12:1–2 (NASB).** [1] Now about that time **Herod the king** laid hands on some who belonged to the church, to do them harm. [2] **And he had James the brother of John executed with a sword**.

Commentary. Up until now, the church was experiencing one exciting conversion after another. First there was Saul of Tarsus, then the Ethiopian eunuch, then Cornelius, and then last week we saw the birth of the first Gentile church in Antioch. When Herod had James killed, it signified a change in the way the Romans were treating the apostles. As we know, Stephen was the first believer to be martyred for his faith. And now James became the first apostle to be martyred. This must have stunned the remaining apostles.

Herod means ruler. That's why there are so many Herod's in the Bible because it's a title and not a name. This Herod was King Herod Agrippa I.

(Q) WHAT DO YOU REMEMBER ABOUT JAMES?_____

(Q) WHAT DO YOU KNOW ABOUT HEROD AGRIPPA I?_____

(Q) ANY OTHER COMMENTS ON THESE VERSES?_____

STOP AND DISCUSS THE ABOVE VERSES AND QUESTIONS. Answers to questions are on the next page.

(Q) WHAT DO YOU REMEMBER ABOUT JAMES?

- James was one of the twelve apostles.
- James was a fisherman (Matthew 4:21–22).
- James had a brother named John, who was also an apostle.
- Jesus nicknamed John and James the **Sons of Thunder** because of their loud and bold personalities (Mark 3:17).
- James's father was Zebedee, and John and James were referred to as the **Sons of Zebedee**.
- James, John, and Peter were Jesus's closest friends and often accompanied Jesus without the other apostles.
- James was with Jesus on the mountaintop when he saw Jesus's transfiguration and then watched Him talk with Moses and Elijah (Matthew 17:1–9).
- James was called to be the leader of the church in Jerusalem (Acts 15:13).

(Q) WHAT DO YOU KNOW ABOUT HEROD AGRIPPA I?

- **Herod Agrippa I.** He was the grandson of Herod the Great and the nephew of Herod Antipas. He had James, the brother of John, beheaded and then threw Peter in jail with the intention of killing him. When an angel of the Lord freed Peter from jail, Herod was so angry, he left Judea and went to Caesarea. While he was in Caesarea giving a speech, the people began yelling, "*He has the voice of a god and not of a man.*" When Agrippa did not "*give God the glory,*" an "*angel of the Lord struck him down*" and then "*he was eaten by worms and died*" (Acts 12).

Here are the other Herods mentioned in the Bible.

- **Herod the Great.** He was king when Jesus was born, and ordered the slaughter of the firstborn boys in Bethlehem in an effort to kill the Messiah.
- **Herod Antipas.** He was king when John the Baptist was beheaded. Later, he declined to pass judgement on Jesus and sent Him back to Pilate (Acts 4). He was also known as **Herod the tetrarch** (Acts 13). He eventually fell out of favor with Rome and was exiled to Gaul.
- **Herod Agrippa II.** He was the son of King Herod Agrippa I and was married to Bernice. Bernice was Agrippa II's sister, who was also previously married to her uncle, Herod Antipas. She was also the sister of Drusilla, who was married to Governor Felix, making Felix and Festus brothers-in-law. King Agrippa II and his wife Bernice were both Jews (Acts 27).

> **Acts 12:3 (NASB).** ³ When [Herod] saw that [James's death] pleased the Jews, he proceeded to arrest Peter as well.

Commentary. It could be argued that James's death was *politically motivated* because when Herod saw that James's death pleased the Jews, he had Peter arrested with the intention of killing him to gain favor with the Jews.

(Q) WHO WERE THE JEWS MENTIONED IN THIS VERSE?_____

(Q) ANY OTHER COMMENTS ON THESE VERSES?_____

STOP AND DISCUSS THE ABOVE VERSES AND QUESTIONS. Answers to questions are on the next page.

> **Acts 12:4 (NASB).** (Now these were the **days of Unleavened Bread**.) ⁴ When [Herod] had arrested [Peter], he put him in prison, turning him over to four squads of soldiers to guard him, intending only after the Passover to bring him before the people.

Commentary. Since Herod had Peter arrested during Passover, this may have been another strategic move to impress as many people as possible since the Passover celebration would be attended by thousands of people from all over the region.

(Q) WHY IS PASSOVER ALSO REFERRED TO AS THE *"Days of Unleavened Bread"*?

_____

(Q) ANY OTHER COMMENTS ON THESE VERSES?_____

STOP AND DISCUSS THE ABOVE VERSES AND QUESTIONS. Answers to questions are on the next page.

> **Acts 12:5 (NASB).** ⁵ So Peter was kept in the prison, but **prayer for him was being made to God intensely by the church.**

Commentary. The NKJV Bible says the *church prayed constantly* for Peter. It sounds like the early church was modeling 1 Thessalonians 5:17 where Paul commanded the church to *"pray without ceasing."*

(Q) WHAT DOES IT MEAN TO *"Pray Without Ceasing"*?_____

(Q) ANY OTHER COMMENTS ON THESE VERSES?_____

STOP AND DISCUSS THE ABOVE VERSES AND QUESTIONS. Answers to questions are on the next page.

ANSWERS TO QUESTIONS FROM THE PREVIOUS PAGE

(Q) WHO WERE THE JEWS MENTIONED IN THIS VERSE?

- Most likely, this was referring to the **Jewish rulers** of the Sanhedrin Council, consisting of the high priests, Pharisees and the Sadducees, but would also include anyone who did not like the Christians.

(Q) WHAT DOES THE *"Days of Unleavened Bread"* REFER TO?

- This refers to the **Passover celebration** when the Israelites eat unleavened bread to remember their Exodus from Egyptian slavery.

  For seven days you shall eat unleavened bread with it, the bread of affliction (for you came out of the land of Egypt in a hurry), so that you will remember the day when you came out of the land of Egypt all the days of your life. (Deuteronomy 16:3)

- Therefore, Herod arrested Peter during the Passover celebration.

(Q) WHAT DOES IT MEAN TO *"Pray Without Ceasing"*?

- It means being aware of God's presence throughout the day.
- It means being content in all circumstances.
- It means realizing our dependence is on God rather than ourselves.
- It means when worry or fear enter our thoughts, we are to turn to prayer and supplication.

> **Acts 12:6–10 (NASB).** [6] On the very night when Herod was about to bring him forward, Peter was sleeping between two soldiers, bound with two chains, and guards in front of the door were watching over the prison. [7] And behold, an **angel of the Lord** suddenly stood near Peter, and a light shone in the cell; and he struck Peter's side and woke him, saying,
> *"Get up quickly."*
> And his chains fell off his hands. [8] And the angel said to him,
> *"Put on your belt and strap on your sandals."*
> And he did so. And he said to him,
> *"Wrap your cloak around you and follow me."*
> [9] And he went out and continued to follow, and yet he did not know that what was being done by the angel was real, but thought he was seeing a vision. [10] Now when they had passed the first and second guard, they came to the iron gate that leads into the city, which opened for them by itself; and they went out and went along one street, and immediately the angel departed from him.

Commentary. An angel supernaturally freed Peter from his chains and then led him through two gates, while four guards were watching him. Obviously, God answered the churches' prayer for Peter.

Why did God allow James to die a terrible death, and yet He spared Peter?

Life is full of questions like this. These are questions we cannot possibly know the answer to because we cannot see all that God sees. Only God knows why He has chosen to allow evil in this world *for a time*.

Prayer works, and in these verses, God answered the churches' corporate prayer. What other types of prayer are there? Give a brief description for each form of prayer.

(Q) CORPORATE PRAYER._____

(Q) PRAYER OF SUPPLICATION._____

(Q) PRAYER OF THANKSGIVING._____

(Q) PRAYER OF INTERCESSION._____

(Q) PRAYING IN THE SPIRIT._____

(Q) ANY OTHER COMMENTS ON THESE VERSES?_____

STOP AND DISCUSS THE ABOVE VERSES AND QUESTIONS. Answers to questions are on the next page.

(Q) CORPORATE PRAYER.

- Corporate prayer is when a group of believers come together to pray at the same time in unity.

  If two of you agree on earth about anything that they may ask, it shall be done for them by My Father who is in heaven. For where two or three have gathered together in My name, I am there in their midst. (Matthew 18:19–20)

- We should guard against corporate prayer turning into gossip.

(Q) PRAYER OF SUPPLICATION.

- Supplication is when we take our requests directly to God.

  Answer me when I call, God of my righteousness! You have relieved me in my distress; Be gracious to me and hear my prayer. (Psalm 4:1)

(Q) PRAYER OF THANKSGIVING.

- Thanksgiving is recognizing what God has already done and remembering to thank Him.
- Thanksgiving is also anticipating what God may do for us in the future.

  Do not be anxious about anything, but in everything by prayer and pleading with thanksgiving let your requests be made known to God. (Philippians 4:6)

(Q) PRAYER OF INTERCESSION.

- Intercession are prayers made on behalf of other people.

  Is anyone among you sick? Then he must call for the elders of the church and they are to pray over him, anointing him with oil in the name of the Lord. (James 5:14)

(Q) PRAYING IN THE SPIRIT.

- When we cannot find the right words to pray, the Holy Spirit will intercede on our behalf.

  When we do not know what to pray for as we should, but the Spirit Himself intercedes for us with groanings too deep for words. (Romans 8:26)

> **Acts 12:11–15 (NASB).** ¹¹ When Peter came to himself, he said,
>   *"Now I know for sure that the Lord has sent forth His angel and rescued me from the hand of Herod and from all that the Jewish people were expecting."*
> ¹² And when he realized this, he went to the house of Mary, the mother of John, who was also called Mark, where many were gathered together and were praying. ¹³ When he knocked at the door of the gate, a slave woman named Rhoda came to answer. ¹⁴ When she recognized Peter's voice, because of her joy she did not open the gate, but ran in and announced that Peter was standing in front of the gate. ¹⁵ They said to her,
>   *"You are out of your mind!"*
> But she kept insisting that it was so. They said, *"It is his angel."*

Commentary. Once Peter was free, he sought safety at Mary's house (mother of John Mark). Mary's home might have been the location of the Last Supper (Luke 22:8–13). Many believers were at Mary's house, praying corporately for Peter. When God answered their prayer, they did not believe it was Peter at the door. ***Does God answer prayer?*** Ask any believer, and you will know the answer. Every changed life of every believer is proof that God answers prayer.

(Q) DESCRIBE A TIME WHEN GOD ANSWERED YOUR PRAYERS._____

(Q) WHAT DO YOU REMEMBER ABOUT JOHN MARK?_____

(Q) ANY OTHER COMMENTS ON THESE VERSES?_____

> **STOP AND DISCUSS THE ABOVE VERSES AND QUESTIONS. Answers to questions are on the next page.**

> **Acts 12:16–17 (NASB).** ¹⁶ But Peter continued knocking; and when they had opened the door, they saw him and were amazed. ¹⁷ But motioning to them with his hand to be silent, he described to them how the Lord had led him out of the prison. And he said,
>   *"Report these things to James and the brothers."*
> Then he left and went to another place.

Commentary. The **James** mentioned by Peter was not the Apostle James who was beheaded at the beginning of this chapter. This James was the half-brother of Jesus.

(Q) WHAT DO YOU REMEMBER ABOUT JAMES, THE HALF-BROTHER OF JESUS?

_____

(Q) ANY OTHER COMMENTS ON THESE VERSES?_____

> **STOP AND DISCUSS THE ABOVE VERSES AND QUESTIONS. Answers to questions are on the next page.**

(Q) DESCRIBE A TIME WHEN GOD ANSWERED YOUR PRAYERS.

- Testimony time.

(Q) WHAT DO YOU REMEMBER ABOUT JOHN MARK?

- He was Barnabas's cousin (Colossians 4:10).
- He wrote the Gospel of Mark.
- He accompanied Paul and Barnabas on their first missionary journey (Acts 13:5). However, he did not complete the trip and abandoned Paul and Barnabas in Pamphylia (Acts 15:38).
- After Barnabas and Saul finished their journey they got into an argument over John Mark and parted ways (Acts 15:39–41).
- Barnabas lived up to his name as an encourager (Acts 4:36) when he mentored John Mark and then took him on his next missionary journey.
- John Mark matured and became a big help during Barnabas's next missionary journey.
- Paul heard about the change in John Mark and asked for him to go on his third missionary journey (2 Timothy 4:11).

(Q) WHAT DO YOU REMEMBER ABOUT JAMES, THE HALF-BROTHER OF JESUS?

- He was a son of Mary and Joseph; therefore, he was the half-brother of Jesus (Matthew 13:55).
- While Jesus was alive, James did not believe Jesus was the Messiah (John 7:2-–5).
- It wasn't until after the resurrection that James turned from being a skeptic to becoming a believer.
- James eventually became a leader in the church in Jerusalem (1 Corinthians 15:7).
- He was the chairman of the Jerusalem Council (Acts 15:13, 19).
- He is the author of the Epistle of James (James 1:1).

> **Acts 12:18–23 (NASB).** ¹⁸ Now when day came, there was no small disturbance among the soldiers as to what could have become of Peter. ¹⁹ When Herod had searched for him and had not found him, he examined the guards and ordered that they be led away to execution. Then he went down from Judea to Caesarea and was spending time there.
> ²⁰ Now he was very angry with the people of Tyre and Sidon; and with one mind they came to him, and having won over Blastus the king's chamberlain, they were asking for peace, because their country was supported with grain from the king's country.
> ²¹ On an appointed day, after putting on his royal apparel, Herod took his seat on the rostrum and began delivering an address to them. ²² The people repeatedly cried out,
> "*The voice of a god and not of a man!*"
> ²³ And immediately an angel of the Lord struck him because he did not give God the glory, and he was eaten by worms and died.

Commentary. Per Roman law, Herod had the guards executed for allowing Peter to escape. Herod was angry because this messed up his plans to execute Peter and gain favor with the Sanhedrin Council. After Peter escaped, Herod went to Caesarea. The Bible does not tell us why he went to Caesarea, but it does say he was angry with the people of Tyre and Sidon. When the people saw Herod was in town, they wanted to make peace with him because they were dependent on grain from Galilee. The people asked Herod's personal servant, Blastus, to set up a meeting with the king.

Herod went all out for the meeting by dressing in his "*royal apparel.*" During the meeting, the people started calling him *god*, and he did not stop them, nor did he give glory to the one true God. Therefore, God struck him, and he died. Remember what God told the Israelites when they made idols? He said, "*I, the LORD your God, am a jealous God*" (Exodus 20:5).

(Q) WAS HEROD AGRIPPA I REALLY EATEN BY WORMS? HOW IS THIS POSSIBLE?

_____

(Q) ANY OTHER COMMENTS ON THESE VERSES?_____

> **STOP AND DISCUSS THE ABOVE VERSES AND QUESTIONS. Answers to questions are on the next page.**

> **Acts 12:24–25 (NASB).** ²⁴ But the word of the Lord continued to grow and to be multiplied. ²⁵ And Barnabas and Saul returned when they had fulfilled their mission to Jerusalem, taking along with them John, who was also called Mark.

Commentary. When Barnabas and Saul (Apostle Paul) returned, we know from Acts 11:30 they brought money from the church at Antioch to give to the church at Jerusalem to buy food during the famine.

(Q) WHAT MISSION DID SAUL AND BARNABAS COMPLETE?_____

(Q) ANY OTHER COMMENTS ON THESE VERSES?_____

> **STOP AND DISCUSS THE ABOVE VERSES AND QUESTIONS. Answers to questions are on the next page.**

(Q) WAS HEROD AGRIPPA I REALLY EATEN BY WORMS? HOW IS THIS POSSIBLE?

- Luke said the source of Herod's illness was worms.
- Modern science has found there are several types of intestinal worms that may be fatal if not treated.

(Q) WHAT MISSION DID SAUL AND BARNABAS COMPLETE?

- They were sent to Antioch by the elders of the church in Jerusalem to confirm salvation had come to the Gentiles in Antioch (Acts 11:22–26).
- They ended up staying in Antioch for a year, discipling the new believers.
- Therefore, they were completing their mission for the Jerusalem church.

Let's RE-Read Tonight's Verses

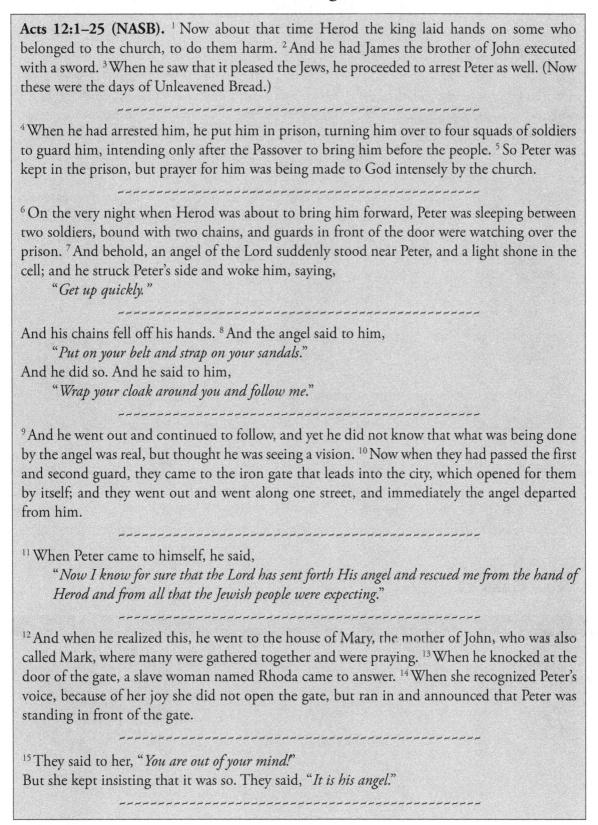

Acts 12:1–25 (NASB). ¹ Now about that time Herod the king laid hands on some who belonged to the church, to do them harm. ² And he had James the brother of John executed with a sword. ³ When he saw that it pleased the Jews, he proceeded to arrest Peter as well. (Now these were the days of Unleavened Bread.)

⁴ When he had arrested him, he put him in prison, turning him over to four squads of soldiers to guard him, intending only after the Passover to bring him before the people. ⁵ So Peter was kept in the prison, but prayer for him was being made to God intensely by the church.

⁶ On the very night when Herod was about to bring him forward, Peter was sleeping between two soldiers, bound with two chains, and guards in front of the door were watching over the prison. ⁷ And behold, an angel of the Lord suddenly stood near Peter, and a light shone in the cell; and he struck Peter's side and woke him, saying,
"*Get up quickly.*"

And his chains fell off his hands. ⁸ And the angel said to him,
"*Put on your belt and strap on your sandals.*"
And he did so. And he said to him,
"*Wrap your cloak around you and follow me.*"

⁹ And he went out and continued to follow, and yet he did not know that what was being done by the angel was real, but thought he was seeing a vision. ¹⁰ Now when they had passed the first and second guard, they came to the iron gate that leads into the city, which opened for them by itself; and they went out and went along one street, and immediately the angel departed from him.

¹¹ When Peter came to himself, he said,
"*Now I know for sure that the Lord has sent forth His angel and rescued me from the hand of Herod and from all that the Jewish people were expecting.*"

¹² And when he realized this, he went to the house of Mary, the mother of John, who was also called Mark, where many were gathered together and were praying. ¹³ When he knocked at the door of the gate, a slave woman named Rhoda came to answer. ¹⁴ When she recognized Peter's voice, because of her joy she did not open the gate, but ran in and announced that Peter was standing in front of the gate.

¹⁵ They said to her, "*You are out of your mind!*"
But she kept insisting that it was so. They said, "*It is his angel.*"

¹⁶ But Peter continued knocking; and when they had opened the door, they saw him and were amazed. ¹⁷ But motioning to them with his hand to be silent, he described to them how the Lord had led him out of the prison. And he said,

"*Report these things to James and the brothers.*"

~~~~~~

Then he left and went to another place. ¹⁸ Now when day came, there was no small disturbance among the soldiers as to what could have become of Peter. ¹⁹ When Herod had searched for him and had not found him, he examined the guards and ordered that they be led away to execution. Then he went down from Judea to Caesarea and was spending time there.

~~~~~~

²⁰ Now he was very angry with the people of Tyre and Sidon; and with one mind they came to him, and having won over Blastus the king's chamberlain, they were asking for peace, because their country was supported with grain from the king's country. ²¹ On an appointed day, after putting on his royal apparel, Herod took his seat on the rostrum and began delivering an address to them. ²² The people repeatedly cried out,

"*The voice of a god and not of a man!*"

~~~~~~

²³ And immediately an angel of the Lord struck him because he did not give God the glory, and he was eaten by worms and died. ²⁴ But the word of the Lord continued to grow and to be multiplied.

²⁵ And Barnabas and Saul returned when they had fulfilled their mission to Jerusalem, taking along with them John, who was also called Mark.

Commentary. Congratulations on finishing the first study on the book of Acts called, **Acts: The Birth of the Church**. We have been reading about how God built His church in Jerusalem and then expanded it into the outer regions of Judea through the power of the Holy Spirit. Christianity was no longer considered a small sect of Judaism, it was now seen as a world-wide religion that was open to everyone, Jews and Gentiles alike.

(Q) Any Final Comments?_____

This is the end of this week's study.

You can follow Peter, James, Barnabas, and Paul on their next adventure in the second study called *Acts: Paul's Three Missionary Journeys.*

ACTS TIMELINE AND PAUL'S LETTERS

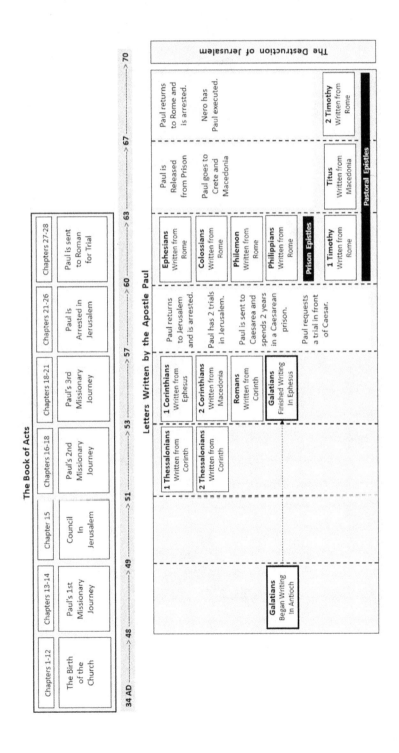

The Book of Acts

Chapters 1-12	Chapters 13-14	Chapter 15	Chapters 16-18	Chapters 18-21	Chapters 21-26	Chapters 27-28
The Birth of the Church	Paul's 1st Missionary Journey	Council In Jerusalem	Paul's 2nd Missionary Journey	Paul's 3rd Missionary Journey	Paul is Arrested in Jerusalem	Paul is sent to Roman for Trial

34 AD ---> 48 ---> 49 ---> 51 ---> 53 ---> 57 ---> 60 ---> 63 ---> 67 ---> 70

Letters Written by the Apostle Paul

Galatians Began Writing In Antioch

1 Thessalonians Written from Corinth

2 Thessalonians Written from Corinth

1 Corinthians Written from Ephesus — Paul returns to Jerusalem and is arrested.

2 Corinthians Written from Macedonia — Paul has 2 trials in Jerusalem.

Romans Written from Corinth — Paul is sent to Caesarea and spends 2 years in a Caesarean prison.

Galatians Finished Writing In Ephesus — Paul requests a trial in front of Caesar.

Ephesians Written from Rome

Colossians Written from Rome

Philemon Written from Rome

Philippians Written from Rome

Prison Epistles

1 Timothy Written from Rome — Paul is Released from Prison / Paul goes to Crete and Macedonia

Titus Written from Macedonia

Pastoral Epistles

2 Timothy Written from Rome — Paul returns to Rome and is arrested. / Nero has Paul executed.

The Destruction of Jerusalem

MAP OF THE MEDITERRANEAN

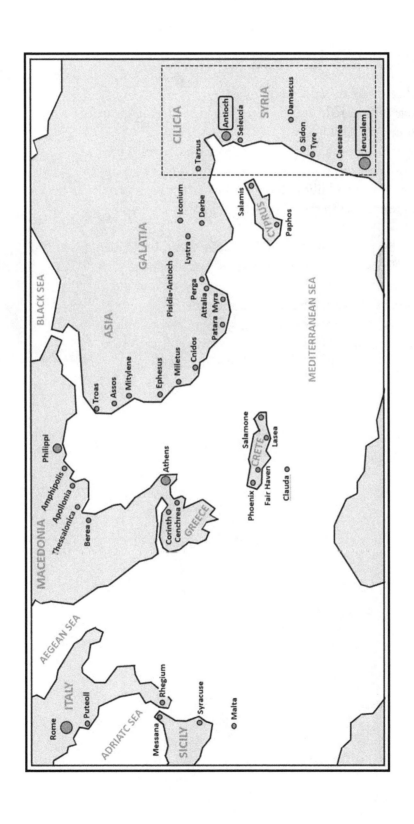

ABOUT THE AUTHOR

Ralph Robert Gomez is a retired software engineer who loves Jesus and came to the Lord later in life.

At the age of thirty-nine years old, while attending graduate school, Ralph had a "*road to Damascus*" experience and has been walking with the Lord since.

Ralph is a native of Colorado and has been married to his high school sweetheart since 1975 and has two children and three grandchildren.

Ralph has been writing Bible studies for the past twenty years and sharing them with his homegroup, the James Gang, and a men's group called the Band of Brothers. In addition, Ralph and his wife have hosted numerous marriage groups over the years and have a passion for helping marriages succeed.

At the urging of his friends and family, Ralph assembled his home group studies into a series of precept Bible studies that challenge the reader to probe deep into God's Word (interpret) and to apply it to their daily life (application), while having fun at the same time!

Ralph's background as an engineer, writing software and technical documents, has uniquely qualified him to use his *analytical skills* to dissect God's Word, verse by verse, making it easy and simple to understand.

CPSIA information can be obtained
at www.ICGtesting.com
Printed in the USA
BVHW021003170123
656424BV00016B/624